ALL IS FORGIVEN, WHEN ROOTED IN LOVE.
COPYRIGHT © 2011 BY TAMEEKA WILLIAMSON

ISBN-10 0-615-50953-3
ISBN-13 9780615509532

ALL SCRIPTURES ARE FROM THE KING JAMES VERSION OF THE BIBLE.

PRINTED IN THE UNITED STATES OF AMERICA.

FOR MORE INFORMATION ABOUT MINISTRIES OR OTHER PUBLICATIONS IN THIS BOOK
PLEASE SEND AN EMAIL TO TAMEEKAWILLIAMSON@HOTMAIL.COM

I

Jeremiah 30:2
Thus speaketh the LORD God of Israel, saying, Write thee all the words that I have spoken unto thee in a book.

(This is the scripture the Lord gave me to write this book)

Content

Some names to people and places have been changed to respect other's privacy

Chapter 1
Growing Pains

*B*rooklyn, New York was my childhood playground. It was about 1985 and the sounds of Boy George, the dances of rappers Salt n Pepa, and shows like He-man and The Facts of Life filled my young world. I was the middle child and I always felt unaccepted by my family. A feeling of "not fitting in" always hovered over me. To add to that I also had a sense of abandonment. It all began to choke my inner voice of who I wanted to become.

I lived at 1009 Lincoln Place with my grandmother, aunt, cousin, uncle, father Daniel and two sisters Kizzy and Nisha. It was a small two bedroom apartment in Crown

Heights. I slept on the floor in the living room with my uncle, dad and sisters. Eventually my sisters and I got a bunk bed and moved into my grandmother's room. One floor up was the apartment belonging to my other aunt, her boyfriend and our three cousins.

My grandmother was born in Trinidad, West Indies. She has five children in total. She worked at Brookdale hospital part-time in the nursing home department. She would bring pudding home for us just about every night. The vanilla was my favorite; it kind of tasted like Bavarian cream filling. She was also a Minister with her own Baptist church. As children my sisters and I had to help clean up and get the church ready for Sunday services. So by the time church started we would be sleeping or playing with our cousins in the back. While I grew up in church, I knew nothing about Jesus from my family directly. Actually I had no personal understanding of any aspect of church or God.

I remember this one time my grandmother took us to a play about the life of Jesus Christ. The only thing that stands out in my memory about the play was the dinner table scene. Jesus said something to the effect of whoever dips in the dish with me will betray me. I thought if everyone saw the person (Judas) dip into the dish with Jesus they should just kill the person before he could actually betray Jesus. All I knew was Jesus was the good guy and the other guy was bad. I had no idea this play was an actual reenactment of what happened many years ago. Afterwards we got to shake the hand of the actor who played Jesus, which at the time seemed really exciting.

Another time we went to see a play about He-man (the 1980's cartoon television icon) that was a very memorable event. One of the characters in the play named Skeletor came down off the stage into the audience and went right up to my younger sister Nisha. It was really funny to me how scared she was. Then tears and screams filled the entire area. I must admit I was a little jealous because I wanted Skeletor to come over to me.

During this time my uncle was addicted to drugs so we saw him whenever he finally came home. He was a charming man with a bright smile. Whenever I saw him he had a funny story to tell me. He would always come home bearing gifts of food usually from Pizza Hut and Kentucky Fried Chicken. My uncle would get the food before the employees threw it out into the trash then bring it home.

My aunt was a teenager at this time with braces. She loved to enforce her rules for us girls whenever she was in charge. Plus she had our teenage cousin as her assistant to help her enforce the rules. They would come up with punishments for us that seemed like torture sometimes. One time they tied my hands to the hallway closet door knob, pulled down my panties, wet a brush and popped my butt with it. Of course it stung my little bottom. However, I am not really sure if the beating stung or their laughter stung me more. Another time we were put in separate rooms and we had to remain in one spot of the room for the entire time. As it turned out I got put into the kitchen (the least exciting room in a home to a child like me). As punishment I had to remain on this one square floor tile. Growing up I was very active so I felt like I was going to die of boredom in that square. I could hear my aunt talking and laughing on the telephone, which made me want to scream.

My sister Nisha, grandmother and I went downtown Brooklyn to a well-known department store. While we

were walking up the stairs a brown skinned male dressed
in a brown security guard uniform approached us. He
told my grandmother that free toys were being given away
downstairs and he offered to take one of us down there to
obtain one, which turned out to be me. As this security
guard escorted me downstairs to the children's department
I followed behind him carelessly. There was a long rack of
clothes on our right side, which he shoved apart then told
me to get in. He stood tall above me, while his eyes gazed
the room left to right as he told me to take off my clothes.
In a squatted position I began to slowly unbutton my top
as I thought of a way to escape from him. When my left
shoulder was about to be exposed he stated, "Hold on" then
after he paused for a moment he continued and said, "Hold
on a minute I think I see a bad guy, stay here!" I whispered
to myself, "You are the bad guy." He began to walk away
and I quickly buttoned my top, he went left and I quietly
ran to the right. Anger and embarrassment ran through my
body as I made my way back to my grandmother and sister.
They were awaiting my arrival at the top of the stairway
where I left them. They questioned where my toy was and
I sharply informed her that they did not have any more. I
never mentioned to my grandmother what that security
guard could have done to me that day. In a way I was
saddened she sent me with that stranger.

Grandmother as we called her was more of a mother
to us growing up. She went to our schools to visit our
teachers, she made all of our meals, she got our clothes
ready for school and she did it all without complaining. On
one hand I believed she took care of us so well because she
loved my dad a lot. On the other hand she probably felt
sorry for us not having our own mother living there with us,
so she became a mother to us.

Most of the time wherever she went, we went too. Other times it was just the three of us children at home alone. We had the best time by ourselves. Being that the front hallway was quite narrow we were able to spread our legs, place our feet on the walls and climb up to the top until our heads touched the ceiling. Then we would jump down. If we did not land correctly on the bottom of our feet it would sting really badly. For three young children the ceiling was extremely high, so that was a big thrill for us. Sometimes we would turn off all the lights in the apartment, get under a sheet and scare ourselves into thinking a monster was inside the apartment chasing us around.

Our father had given us a specific route to use when walking to school and back home. However one day we decided to start taking a new way home after school. Needless to say my father saw us walking our new route one afternoon. When we got home our butts were in a lot of trouble and headed for an inevitable spanking. We actually tried to change routes two more times. Clearly we did not learn our lesson the first time. Punishment for getting caught would be too severe so we determined it would be best to stick to our father's route after all.

The mornings that we were late to school, I would always ask my older sister Kizzy to walk me into my classroom. You see after being teased about my long chin, pointy nose and wide feet by my aunt and cousin I was extremely insecure and shy about being the focus of attention in any crowded environment. So when we would get to the door of my classroom and I looked inside I only saw a sea of children ready to stare at me and I would panic. Just the thought of opening the classroom door, seeing the eyes from the stares of the students, then having to walk through the classroom to my desk, while the teacher asked me why I was late was overwhelming to me. I tried to open the door then I would see the eyes, so I would beg and cry for my sister to wait for a second so I could get up enough courage to go inside the classroom. After doing that about four to five times she would say she had to get to her own class and threaten to leave me there. Finally she would have to surprisingly knock on the door, quickly run and leave me with no other option but to go inside. When she would knock on the door all the children turned their heads to the window in the classroom door and I was so frightened I could not even run away. Walking from the door to my desk was long and painful. The last time I remember being late my sister became so annoyed with my begging and crying that after the normal attempts instead of surprisingly knocking on the door she just left me there. After she was gone I tried to go into the classroom on my own but fear had a stronghold on my mind. That day I never made it into my class but I was not faced with the sea of eyes looking at me and it seemed worth it. Walking throughout the school I made my way to my sister's class. I signaled her to come out; she asked to go to the bathroom and met me outside. She was upset because she saw that I still had my book bag and had not made it into my class. I started begging her to stay in the hallway with me after she tried telling me again to get into my class, ultimately she left me again. That was a day to remember.

Academically I was somewhat of an honor student. I had awards in the principal's office but I was so shy and fearful I hardly spoke inside the classroom. At home I was thought of as the one in charge. Everyone thought I was such a rude and out of control child. Actually I would say that I was simply the most outspoken of the children. Whatever my sisters and I secretly discussed, I openly said. Which I guess made me the focus of attention in a very negative way. That attention led me to be the one that received the punishment for our views. The real issue wasn't me saying such a terrible thing; the issue was my family being from Trinidad was very strict about children not voicing their own opinion.

After my spoken thoughts were constantly being subjected to repression, I shut down emotionally. As a child you yearn for the approval of your parents and it was clear to me I was a big disappointment to them. The first thing my father did when he came home from work was beat me for misbehaving and my mother was not there giving me the nourishment all children need. My aunt and cousin teased us about my mother not being around and her not wanting to deal with us "bad children". Their emphasis was mainly directed towards me. At the time the things that were said were by teenagers forced to babysit three small children. In those moments their age did not matter to me, all I heard and felt was "Jah-see was a bad child and her mother did not want to deal with her". Their lack of understanding the needs of children played a major role in how we were subject to live. Instead of going to the playground to explore and burn off our energy in a constructive manner we were inside that small apartment a lot of the time. They failed to realize we needed (mainly me) more physical playtimes. Most of my overly active behavior was misunderstood as being out of control and labeled "bad". I know my grandmother and father were too busy working to supply us with the intimate time we desperately needed.

Believing my mother Beth did not even desire to be with her daughter and my father was always disciplining me out of anger made me feel rejected and definitely unwanted. Being teased for how my body was designed created such doubt inside of my mind about my outer beauty. I wet the bed for a very long time growing up. One of the reasons was

the dark was terrifying to me, but my family thought I was
just being lazy. While watching television I heard someone
say children sometimes wet the bed due to insecurities within
themselves. This to me sounded like my main reason for
wetting the bed.

One of my outlets was school in many ways. On the
playground I was accepted by the little boys and my teachers
adored my academic ability. Kevin was my first boyfriend
and he gave me my first kiss in the second grade. He also
had another girlfriend secretly so I decided to get a different
boyfriend. This other boy was the opposite of Kevin; he was
quiet and soft spoken. By the third grade I met the new boy
in school named Walter. He became my boyfriend and the
second boy that kissed me. The kiss was a peck on the lips,
for us having a boyfriend or girlfriend was fairly innocent.
We simply passed notes that said "hello" and we told our
friends we had a boyfriend or girlfriend. Now it is really funny
because most of the time we did not speak to each other after
the big official commitment. Sometimes during school all the
children would assemble in the auditorium where we watched
a movie. This day Walter and I sat together and he went
beyond the boundaries my past two boyfriends had gone.
Being that it was dark he placed his hand down my pants
underneath my butt and we sat that way the entire assembly.

A wonderful feeling of joy and acceptance came over
me whenever I was showed attention by these boys. The exact
feelings I needed from my family that I lacked. Television
was another outlet for me. I watched a lot of it especially
late at night. The caressing and kissing on television plus the
attention at school naturally made intimate relationships very
appealing to me. Those images I saw on television seemed like
expressions of love. To see those same images expressed to me
by those two boys made me feel what I then knew love to be.

My mother came by or called once in a while. I would anxiously wait for her to surprise us at school with one of her quick visits. She came to the school around four or five times and I loved seeing her for those short moments. Her problems with drugs kept her from being able to be there for us a lot more. The only memories of my mom before living at Lincoln place are few. When we went to Trinidad at the age of three, a house lamp had fallen on the lower part of my right leg; I still have the scar today. I do not remember my mother comforting me at that time. Also there was the night before we were going back to the states, I was running and fell into a sewer wearing an all-white outfit. Fortunately, I do not recall the beating my mother said she gave me.

By the time I was in the fourth grade we moved into a four bedroom house with a basement in Jamaica, Queens. At first I missed Brooklyn so much that before I went to sleep I imagined playing at recess with my friends. When I started school I was still a little shy. A group of boys in my new class began messing with me. Sometimes my coat would be thrown on the floor and stepped on inside the closet. When I turned around to check the class for the culprit one boy from the group would be looking at me laughing. Needless to say it was his doing and he continued to do it until I became fed up and threw his coat on the floor. I then either ripped it or spat on it. When he went to the closet I did not turn around I just listened for his reaction and it came across the room loud and clear. He yelled at the whole class, "Who did this to my jacket?" No one answered his question and my coat never hit the floor again. That summer I found out that one boy from the group liked me and wanted me to be his girlfriend. When he was not with his friends this all came out of course. He was the quiet one out the group whenever they did something childish to me he would softly laugh, I only remember hearing him speak twice. The feeling was not mutual and I was satisfied with knowing he liked me. Years later after we moved I was visiting my old neighborhood friends when the boy that made all the funny jokes about me and tormented my coat told me they all liked me including him. So now he wanted to hook up with me, but I could not get passed how he treated me as a child. He was a good looking young man and him wanting to be with me and me not taking him up on his offer made me feel great. That was my sweet revenge.

Our friend that lived across the street had some new house guests, his ghetto cousins moved in. Being that I was from Brooklyn when he became part of our family he heard stories about my bad behavior. He was out to prove Brooklyn was not better than Queens, by me fighting his ghetto male cousin. I avoided fighting this boy for a good while. We were not allowed to play outside of our yard often so they would come by trying to get me to come out and fight. About two times I was in front of my yard and I went back in just not to fight him. They thought I was scared and I began to get upset because I began to look like a punk to them. I always thought I could hurt someone if I fought them hard enough. With all the karate movies I watched I thought I would come out swinging uncontrollably. Then one day I was sitting on my father's parked car in front of the yard when my so called friend, his cousin and their other family members snuck up on me. By the time I saw them I could not go into the yard so I stood there and this chump actually hit a girl so I was not about to punk out. I whipped that boy tail so bad his own cousin started laughing and teasing him. After that we fought about five more times just so he could try and redeem himself, but every time he shamefully loss. When

13

school started he enrolled and was placed in my fifth grade class. On his first day he got into a fight and again got his butt whipped. I began to feel bad for him because he had a few more fights after that and loss them all.

One day my grandmother sent the three of us to live with our mother when I was eleven before consulting my father about it. We were so excited to finally be living with her. She had a train apartment, which was long and you had to go through one room to get to the others. The coolest part was moving back to Brooklyn, the saddest part was leaving without saying goodbye to my father. My sister Kizzy and I shared the second bedroom. I was supposed to sleep on the top bunk but I was still very much scared of the dark. Often times I woke up in her bed. It would take me about an hour at the least just to fall asleep.

For a while my other grandmother Katherine lived with us. Now this was great for me because I finally had someone that gave me all of the attention and love that I craved so dearly as a child. Before school she would tell me to walk with her to the bus stop. When her bus came she would put a ten or twenty dollar bill in my hand, then get on the bus for work. Next I would walk to the store to get change for my bus to school. Yes, I loved the favoritism and the cash was great too. When my mother was high on drugs, her and my grandmother would argue about the favoritism towards me. My mother was hurt because she was not my grandmother's favorite child. That made me sad for my mother. I sometimes thought that was the reason she began using drugs to get away from all her inner pain. I recall one time when they were arguing my mother stated she does not have any favorite children because it is not right. My insides flipped about four times. If my sisters were not her favorite she sure had me fooled. She actually told me the only reason my grandmother

14

favored me was because I looked like my dad and she always liked him.

After my grandmother went on a trip to Florida and only brought me back gifts, my heart began to change towards her. No one else received any gifts and it made my mother upset and my sisters simply said, "She didn't get us anything." I could see it hurt their feelings because I knew that look of disappointment quite well. The only option I had to spare my sisters the pain they were feeling or would eventually feel was by me withdrawing myself away from my grandmother. Soon afterwards my grandmother moved out of the apartment. I guess my mother's drug abuse and their arguing began to be too much for her.

Being home alone was not anything foreign to us, but being alone for days at a time and hungry was very new to us. By 1991 my mom was still battling with her drug addiction demon. When we first moved in I thought she would stop using drugs for us. I could see that was not going to happen and it felt more and more like she still did not care about us. Resentment, anger and bitterness began to build up inside of me towards her. Then sadness came because it was like she was not in control. Those drugs were an awful weapon that destroyed the souls of the users and the people that loved them.

Doing whatever she had to, to support her habit affected me. One time she had taken us all school shopping for brand new clothes. We were so happy, but of course it was too good to be true. She came in the middle of the night and took all the clothes, every piece and sold them to get high. Once again I did not have anything decent to wear to school of my own. I had to continue borrowing my sister's clothes. What happened to my new favorite "Color

Me Badd" music group tee shirt and all the other new clothes was the question I asked my sister. She was a bit upset in her response but she rarely showed her anger. "She sold it!" Well I had a follow up question for that. What she sold it for? My mind did not even register a reason. With a hint of sarcasm and hurt in her voice she said, "What you think she sold it for?" Then it hit me, how could I be so dumb, she sold it for drugs.

Well it was back to my ragged shirts and borrowed jeans. I was the only one who had to ride the bus to school and on top of that I had to pay half price. For me that meant I had to endure an hour long walk or forty-five minutes if I walked through Marcy projects. Either my mother was not home to give me fifty-five cents or most of the time she did not have it. Sometimes I would jump the turnstile at the train station. I did not like doing that too much because the kids from LG or Lafayette Garden projects rode the train. The group of kids that generally rode the train were loud and troublemakers, none of which I enjoyed being around.

All these mishaps were just building a case of resentment in my mind against my mother. Wishing I lived with my mother began to leave a real bitter taste in my mouth. Be careful what you ask for was becoming my new familiar phrase. Then there was a boy at school that teased me about my mother being on drugs, he was one of the LG projects train riders. I realize now that he was a child, but at the time I could not see that aspect of the situation. His uncle was a drug dealer in LG, so he felt the need to inform me that my mother performed oral sex to get drugs from him. At the end of the day I did not care what she did or what anyone thought about her, she was my mother and I knew that if she did do that it was only because she was sick. I always believed one day she would get better. In the meantime I was still suffering the brutal blows of her addiction. As a result, I had challenges expressing my thoughts and feelings openly to the level that I desired.

A popular boy from LG projects asked me to be his girlfriend and it was a surprise to me. I was not a pretty, overly attractive or popular girl like my sister Kizzy. So it made me extremely happy to be recognized as being pretty in his sight. Plus my sister's boyfriend was his best friend and now I was able to hang out with her more often. I was twelve years old insecure and I chased my sister around like she was my god. We rarely went into the project buildings, but this summer day we were in someone's apartment. There was myself, my boyfriend who was about fourteen years old, Kizzy and another person I am not too sure of. As my sister sat in the living room with the unknown male we went to the back room of the apartment.

We sat on the bed and he kissed me on the lips I was so nervous even though his mouth was closed, I had only been kissed when I was in the second grade. He laid me down on the bed, while continuing to kiss me without me kissing him back. The bed was positioned against the wall with dark red sheets, I was lying flat on my back when he began to unbutton my pants and gently pull them off. He stood up beside the bed so I slightly turned my head to see what he was doing. He was removing his pants and underwear before getting back onto the bed to spread my limp legs apart. I laid there with a single tear rolling off my left eye and as I mustarded up the words to say, "Stop", he mumbled a response, but continued on. I repeated my fearful statement of "Stop", once more then he got up and motioned me to get dressed. What just happened? My vision was somewhat blurred and my hearing was faint as I walked three steps through to the opened bathroom door. I washed my face and before I could grasp my next thought my sister came in the bathroom and asked did I have sex with him? That was it? I had sex? It felt like rape! On television the women did not cry afterwards like I wanted to do. I am not sure what my response to that question was from my sister. After I walked out of that bathroom we left the apartment and I stayed as far away from those projects and that boy as possible. I lost my virginity at twelve years old and I felt so disgusted and tainted. Who could I express all of these high and low emotions to? I began to feel more and more alone mentally, burying my feelings seemed like the only option.

I heard a psychologist say that what your parents did to you was not your fault. Well if that was true then why did she leave us all back then? Why is she now with my sisters and not with me? Phone calls would often times go unanswered or unreturned. I have yet to receive a birthday cake from her but my sisters received a birthday cake many times. If I keep focusing on these negatives I could go on and on. I have to believe the best. I just remind that little girl inside me that she has been busy and does not mean to hurt my feelings. Then I think about when the Lord told me, "Nothing shall hurt you, unless you let it hurt you." So I chose not to let anything hurt me past, present or future.

When we were sent away to live in Brooklyn, my grandmother and aunt left shortly after, leaving my father the house. He remained in that house for a couple of years with his girlfriend and my new sister. I bounced around after my mother threw me out for as she phrased it "being too disrespectful" then from my grandmother's place, to my aunt's place to some nights back at my mother's. My family genuinely loved me, but I could not receive their method of love during that stage of my life. My mind could not comprehend why anyone would love a person their own mother did not love. I was mildly suicidal, rebellious and rude to everyone because I lacked understanding and was full of anger. Even in ending all my pain I was too weak and fearful to follow through with several knife threats on myself. My father never forced me to live with him and that choice was not high on my list. I loved my father, but by fourteen I was too free willed and undisciplined from living with my mother for that short time and moving around so much. He was the total opposite of my mother and although I wanted restraints his were too tight. I continued bouncing back and forth physically and mentally.

When I was about fifteen years old, for my mother to gain housing placement in a larger apartment she asked me to accompany her to a homeless shelter. As it turned out I had to reside at the shelter with my family, which was not part of our initial conversation. We went from a Bronx shelter to a Queens's shelter to another Queens's shelter. It was a roller coaster ride and I was ready to get off. After a three day disappearance by my mother I had an opportunity to exit the unwanted ride I found myself on.

Chapter 2 Group Home Living

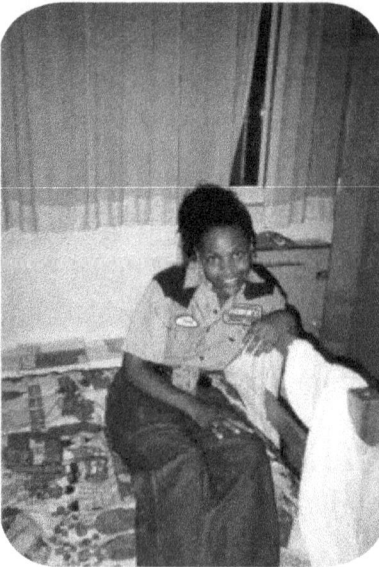

The wild ride was over and my next stop was the Agency Operating Boarding Home (A.O.B.H.). "Group home" was the common name throughout the neighborhood. There were six girls including myself and three regular female staff. The staff stayed at the house with us for two to three days at a time, in a rotating schedule. Isis Boulevard Group Home was the name of our boarding home in Jamaica Queens. Our reputation was the best throughout the agency. Most of the girls in our house were good students in school and not known for being undisciplined like the girls in the other homes. A lot of the other girls in the other group homes had drug problems, had been raped and homeless. I was very fortunate to be placed in such an uncommon home. Lynn was on duty the night I arrived at Isis around 10pm on October 16th 1996.

Lynn was so in tuned with the girls I initially thought she was a resident. I remember the front door was open and being able to see through the screen porch door while the lady rang the doorbell. One of the girls and Lynn were sitting on the living room couch watching television when I was dropped off. The house looked like a real home and later on it became exactly that to me.

We all thought of Lynn as the mother of the house. Whenever we had a problem we would mostly run to her for advice. She told us whenever something happened we should also view the situation from the other person perception. Before we learned that principle we just blamed the other person for whatever happened and only said what wrong they did towards us. "Everything happens for a reason" was her favorite quote. I believe she used it so much we would never wallow in a problem and we focused on what good would come out of any situation. Lynn was clever in that way of not making us feel discouraged whenever we made an immature decision. Understanding how to handle our different personalities made it easy for her to parent us all.

I would lay in the bed with Lynn and tell her how I felt as a child not having the type of relationship with my own mother as I had with her. She would tell me not to blame myself for the decisions of other people and allow what has not killed me to make me stronger. It was in those moments that I began to understand why my mother lived the way she did. So I finally quit blaming my birth for being too much for my mother to handle. I also recognized that her mother did not raise or approve of her. This was part of how she became who she was. I was determined to not allow my mishaps keep me in a cycle of mishaps. I desired to get as far away from my past as possible. Lynn would

21

take us to her family and friends' homes because to her we were her daughters. Her only son was at Isis with us a lot of the time when she was on duty. She gave us driving lessons and always encouraged us to be the best us that we could be.

Another staff member was Stacy; she was the church lady to us. She had a beautiful singing voice and I never heard her curse. She did not use profanity and that showed me her strength, love and respect for the Lord. This was commendable to me especially because everyone in the house cursed like sailors and she never caved in under pressure. Making us laugh with her impersonations of Martin Lawrence was her specialty. Stacy was adopted as a child and has not met her biological family yet. She understood my desire to meet my mother's fourth child, a baby girl born in April of 1988. She had been taken by the state of New York due to my mother's drug addiction. My paternal grandmother took us to the foster care agency once to see her when she was about three or four years of age.

One time Stacy was being questioned about her faith and not in a way for the person to receive understanding. At first I was laughing and co-signing the person's doubts about the Bible. Actually I did not have a clue about what was in the Bible, but that did not stop me from agreeing on a topic I had no knowledge of. Then I asked Stacy how could a new book (the New Testament) be written after the old one was already written? I do not really remember her answer, mainly because it did not help me understand the Bible any more than before I asked.

Then there was Ursula who we referred to as our sex education mentor. Blasting Lil' Kim songs while we drove around in her green Camry was pleasurable for teenage girls. We always asked her about our sexual curiosities or solutions to sexual problems. Two staff members were from Queens and the third one was from Long Island. Ursula was more of a friend type of mother to us. Whenever we did not do what we were told she would fuss with us like one of our friends would. She had a crush on my father which was funny because she was so open about her sexuality. It didn't seem like a match made in heaven but I would not have disapproved of her being my stepmom.

However Jesus Christ never came up in my discussions about God with them. At the time I do not believe their faith in Christ would have made much of an impact in my life. My reason for saying that is because although the ladies did not lead terrible lives I did not see Christ being their first love. To me a person of God leads a life that clearly exemplified the life of who they were following. So if I knew a person that said they loved God, but smoked I did not believe they really loved God. To me if you loved God so much and He loved you why were you still addicted to smoking? Or being lazy? Or having sex with someone other than your husband? Or being overweight? If your God was such a good God why couldn't He help you be better in those situations? These were my inward questions to people that said they loved God but clearly was not changing their imperfections in their lives. It is funny how even when you're not living for Jesus you know the difference between right and wrong.

I had the pleasure of speaking with Ursula in May of 2007 about how I was never taught anything from Christians about Jesus Christ. I did not know God on a personal level. I read a scripture once in a while growing up and I saw some biblical movies. Still, I had no personal connection to God and I was a bit turned off from a God that wanted all the praise and attention. After all He did not

keep my mom from leaving me, being a crack head nor did
He feed me when my stomach was empty. Yet He wanted
me to praise Him with thanks. That was not going to
happen. I was not satisfied with His so called service thus
far.

Ursula's view was that everything happens for a
reason and God probably did not want me to know that
stuff at the time. I then had to explain to her although to
everything there is a season and a time, we were all made
to worship and fellowship with God. To me, God would
not keep the very thing from me that He created me for. I
believe some people missed their opportunity to strengthen
me with knowledge and understanding of the loving God
they followed. Even with them not teaching me about
Jesus, I did not see their lives being completely laid down
to the extent that I would have changed my lifestyle. Today
I know God draws us with loving kindness, so for me to
have more understandable detailed knowledge about Jesus
would have been kind. As people that believe in Jesus
Christ our actions are not supposed to be opposite of what
we tell others God desires us to do. A good God would not
purposely delay me knowing Him. He placed people in my
life to show and tell me about His goodness. Some of those
people failed to deliver the message in a way I could receive
it. Are they going to hell for that? No, I'm not saying that,
however they could have planted a seed through their
actions because that was what I focused on. Does everyone
have to be perfect to be a believer? No, but everyone should
be eager to change their way of living to better represent the
good God they are following so that the people watching
will desire to follow Him too.

A month before first arriving at Isis I turned 16
years old. I remember myself and two of my sisters, one

was 5 and the other was 14 and we were all driven from Manhattan to Queens with our bags in a white van. My youngest sister Princess was dropped off first, I could not do anything but hide my tears because my other sister Nisha was already crying and I wanted to be the strong one. It was at that moment that I felt like I made the wrong decision. It started with us being in a shelter with our mother. She was still on drugs and had left us in the shelter for three days without them knowing. When they finally realized she was gone, we thought we should tell the truth about her drug addiction. I believe I was more ready to tell the truth than my sister because a few nights earlier a woman from the shelter went with me to find my mother. I knew her hang out spots on Lexington Avenue in Brooklyn near LG projects. I never forgot how my mother reacted to us coming out there. My heart ached to be rejected again by her. I heard the woman ask her if she wanted to come back to the shelter with us. She shook her head no and the woman began pleading with her. It was obvious my mother was high on drugs because her mannerisms became as a wounded child. She would talk about her childhood pains and the love she desired from her own mother. Whenever she did that she would cry and I would begin to cry myself. This late night on Lexington Avenue I just wanted her to forget about her past and know that I loved her. Why couldn't we just be what she used to ease her pain? That was the first time I saw her decide when given the choice of drugs or us that she openly chose drugs. So we left and the train ride was shared in tears between a woman who could not understand why another woman left her children and a teenage girl with a deep scar of rejection.

I answered the people at the shelter and simply said, "She's on drugs." I was so ashamed and embarrassed not for myself but for the image of my mother. After my five year old sister was dropped off it was my turn and then my fourteen year old sister did not want to let me go, nor did I want to leave. She began crying again and I tried not to cry, but I felt her pain. We had lost our mother and now it was as if we were losing each other. I wanted a better life for them and for myself. I did not want them to witness what I did that night on Lexington Avenue. Being teased at school about your mother being on drugs or not having school clothes because she sold them to get high, none of that was in the future I imagined for them. So I had to be strong and stand by my decision.

My roommate was a Hispanic girl from Manhattan. She was quiet for the most part, but when she spoke it was either a joke in ignorance or totally flipping out at a staff member. "Frank" was the name of her mysterious boyfriend. A man we never meet face to face. It turned out he was much older than her, had another girlfriend and was abusive to her at times. My boyfriend at the time was the total opposite. However later on in life my boyfriend became "Frank" in so many ways. My new roommate went to Benjamin Cardozo high school, which was a short bus ride away from our house. Traveling an average of two hours or more one way to Brooklyn was becoming a strain on me. So I decided to start over at a new school with a new mind set. I made up classes in after school, night school and summer school due to cutting every day with my sister and friends. That still was not enough to graduate on time. I transferred into Cardozo and my roommate transferred out. I believe she left to obtain her G.E.D. I am not for certain as to why she was at the group home and it remains a mystery to me. The only thing I really remember her talking to me about was her boyfriend. Mostly asking me if he called or to inform me he was on his way over to pick her up. It seemed as if she was not into letting people in her mental world. That relationship taught me how to live with a person who expressed little and still be able to love them for who I wished them to become. She was the second girl to leave Isis. She moved to the group home Nisha lived at.

The little petite dark skinned Honduran - American from Manhattan was a very generous and sensitive person to the people she loved. She was the only person in the house with total privacy because she had her own private room. We called ourselves sisters but argued all the time. Everyone in the house thought we were a couple. The problem was I wanted to be free from being a big sister and she was quite needy. Whenever she came crying to me about things I thought they were stupid a lot of the times. We would argue because she would keep letting people, boys mostly hurt her feeling over and over. At the time I was very selfish. I felt like I had my own problems and she should just toughen up. I guess looking back at it now I was weaker than what I perceived her to be. My feelings got hurt very easily also, we just handled it differently. She would cry and whine to us about people then put those same people right back in a position to hurt her again. On the other hand, I would cry mostly in the shower or at night before bed. I would keep it to myself then leave the people that hurt me alone. These people that hurt us were also friends and family, not just boys. Deep down inside I wanted to get out all my thoughts and feelings like she did. Not being courageous or strong enough to let others see my emotions held me in the weaker category. As a child her mother had done some mean things to her, mostly because her mother was an alcoholic. Growing up with three younger brothers she learned how to use her feisty mouth to get her point across. I believe she had that little people's syndrome. That's the syndrome when you have a big mouth, big car or big ego to compensate for your little height. As an entertainer she had a place to escape from her past and present problems.

Across the hall from her was the youngest girl in the house she was from the Bronx and loved making jokes. Being quite developed physically for her age and wearing glasses she was also a bit loud. She was a teen with an opinionated spirit which had to be hard for her mother to deal with. Their lack of cohabitating together and her constantly running away lead to a PINS warrant. Person In Need of Supervision is what PINS stands for. Her mother had one issued for her which led her to the group home. Maybe around April of 1998 her mother decided it was time for her to return home. We were all quite sad to see her leaving us. I quickly realized she was not my family; none of us were for that matter. We could be moved at any time or our parents could get us back if they wanted. That was hard to swallow because I felt like they were my family. When someone left it was just not the same, even though we said we would visit her and she said she would visit us. This was especially difficult with us being teenagers with feelings of rejection and abandonment. In my mind it was only a matter of time before everyone else I loved in the house would leave me alone again. My plan to leave before they did began after that.

The biggest bedroom in the house was occupied by the two final girls. We viewed one of the girls as being dingy. She was from Manhattan and was very immature. However we knew that she was just putting on an act most of the time for the staff. She was the third girl to leave because she became pregnant. Some would say her roommate Kathy was an adult trapped in a teenager's body. She thought she was more mature than everyone else.

Being that Kathy was originally from Brooklyn I completely understood why. My first morning at Isis, Kathy made me a raisin bagel for breakfast. However for some reason she did not speak to me after that. We walked by each other like the other person was not even there for a couple of months. Staff was curious as to why we were not speaking and I was too. Today she says she does not remember why we did not speak. My guess is she ran the house before I got there, probably did not perceive any of the other girls to be a threat to her and she gladly carried that Brooklyn confidence like a handbag. Then here I came, a Brooklyn native and I definitely brought my "A" game (best attitude). So of course she perceived me as a threat to a home she had on lock down. After no communication and talk of us throwing blows, we were tag teaming everything and everybody. Two Brooklyn egos being under one roof was a lot for everyone else to deal with.

In 1998 Kathy and I was on a mission to defy all the group home rules before anyone else left the Isis family. By this time I had convinced the little Honduran girl to move into the room across the hall and I moved into her single private room. One late night while the other girls were on their weekend family or boyfriend visits, our boyfriends came by for an overnight visit. They had to jump onto the backdoor's covering to get into my bedroom window. Even though the rules stated our doors could not be locked without staff having access, mine was. I had taken the key to my door off the staff keychain. They had so many keys I could have left my key on and they would not have found it in a timely manner anyway. Coincidently that night we learned our boyfriends went to high school together for a little while before I relocated to the group home and before he left for Florida. So our sneak over with them was not uncomfortable, it was a funny and a surprising reunion.

The second sneak over was from our two main neighborhood friends from around the corner. They were best friends and you rarely saw one without seeing the other. Being at our house was a daily routine for them. This weekend I believe we were the only girls' home again. We were all flirting as usual and began playing truth or dare with ice cream and kisses. We were being our usual devious selves but they took the flirting seriously. So we asked did they want to sneak in and stay for the rest of the night. That's when the prophylactic jokes began which at the time I did not understand what they were referring to. However no prophylactics were going to be necessary because we were not planning on going that far with them. Having another sneak over was our goal for that night. Just breaking the rules and knowing we were so good that we could not get caught was our reward. All of this steamed from our big Brooklyn egos. Our saying was "Please, I'm from Brooklyn" or "I'm from B.K." Our minds were set that we could do anything because we were from Brooklyn. Also so much had tried to break us that did not succeed.

Then we started making homemade videos. One video we tied up a girl that lived at Isis and left her in the dark. We set up a hidden camera on another girl having a conversation with her boyfriend. They were caught talking about sex that they said they were not having. Another time we did a karaoke video with songs from Biggie Smalls, Destiny Child, plus a few made up McDonalds and yeast infection commercials. Then there was the time a couple of the girls including myself decided to make a sneaking out the house video, around one o'clock in the morning. We made 1998 a very memorable year before we split up for our adult life adventures. That year we also went on Jamaica Avenue and got our bodies tattooed. I got marked with a drama symbol (a happy and sad face) onto my right arm.

My Brooklyn buddy was not new to tattoos. She already had a spider web tattoo around her naval. The day we went she got two panthers with Gemini written underneath in Arabic on her arm. Although she was raised mostly in Brooklyn she later moved to Queens with her mother and two brothers. Her and her mother argued a lot, which led to her mother filing a PINS warrant against her. When the police picked her up she was at home in her room. With the group home being close to her mother's house she got even by still hanging out with the people her mother disagreed with.

Attending my prom was not an appealing occurrence until the group home staff urged me to go. Everyone's prom day became a special event at our house and I am glad I made the decision to give them and myself the memories. No matter the problems we had becoming one; we became the family we all yearned for on the inside. Even through the problems we had becoming ourselves; we all loved each other at the end of that time of being together. That became a time of growing together and growing up.

My questions after this life changing experience were…
Why did it have to end?

Why did I meet such great, helpful people only for them to be taken away from me?

It was like a reoccurring nightmare of having a taste of love that leaves. I could not understand why I was on my own and alone. My feelings were not of joy. I was literally scared to become an adult. I feared failing at life and the inevitable of failing at love.

Chapter 3
Sex and
Destruction

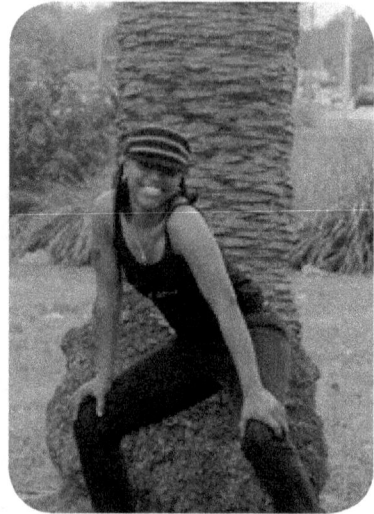

*A*fter high school I left the group home to join the US navy. My primary reason for wanting to join was to make a better life for myself and secondary to get out of New York. Unfortunately college was not really an option. I was informed that me going to college was not going to be possible due to my grade point average (GPA) being too low. From what I remember it was around 1.0. Of course I put the blame on my high school guidance counselor. I felt betrayed because I was always in her office speaking with her about my grades and school.

With me being around my counselor so much why wouldn't she tell me the importance of going to class and making good grades? It was probably because I already knew I should be going to all my classes and we both knew I was more than capable of making good grades. In actuality, she did tell me to go to my classes and use my full potential. I did not heed to her correction because I was having fun and did not understand the severity of my actions. I had no idea your grades played a role in getting into college. I thought you graduate high school and go to college. That was partially my own ignorance. Later I found out I could go to a community college and take remedial classes to bring me up to the college learning level. However I did not desire to get into debt with student loans and I was not ready to pay for college out of my own pocket.

While in the navy I was so home sick. It had been my first time away from New York and my family. My sister Kizzy (the one I was always with) did not even write me one letter. I was so hurt and angry at her for treating me the way I felt my mother treated me. She was the closest person to me in my life at that time along with my so called boyfriend who was in college and he wrote me once or twice. I think I received about three letters my entire stay at Great Lakes after sending off probably ten letters to people. One of my good friends did not even write me but her mother did write me a very lovely letter. The letter was telling me she was very proud of me for graduating high school and doing something good with my life. She later died in 2003 from a battle with throat cancer. She was the first person to pass away that I really knew personally and loved.

I remember when I got my first chance to call home I called the group home and spoke to Ursula. All I could do was cry because I wanted to leave. Loneliness kicked in and all those feelings that Mr. Lonely brings came right along with him, sadness, fear, anger and anxiety. She told me I would be okay and not to be sad and not to cry. Those were not her exact words but that was basically what she told me.

My mother had been off drugs and she had an apartment with her boyfriend in Brooklyn. She even had a job working at a Laundromat. She had finally gotten her life back in a way. I was very happy for her achievements. Growing up I would say, "She will get off those drugs one day." So to finally see it was wonderful. When I wrote her a letter it came back return to sender. I was devastated to think that she was back on drugs and had lost her apartment. Yes my mind went to the extreme to have thought she lost her apartment, her daughter and life again. I wrote one of my sisters asking what was going on with my mother but I never got a response back from her with the answer. This definitely did not help ease my mind.

I took full responsibility for me not being there to watch my mother and was certain that was the cause of her being back on drugs? Why did I feel the need to leave New York to make a better life for myself when I had a family I should be helping? It seemed to me that I was being selfish. These were all so called reasons and excuses to quit boot camp and go back to what I knew to be familiar. Actually I now believe my mind was looking for a reason to leave because I was not able to get the military job I wanted. Fear began to cover my mind. Being on a ship at sea for six months at a time did not seem appealing to me. Then of course I began to blame my recruiter for not being totally honest with me about the military. Once again it was my own ignorance and anxiousness to leave New York to become someone my family and I would be proud of.

We would wake up about four or five in the morning to work out or as they called it "get smoked". This was around September of 1998 and it was colder than any weather I felt in New York. What started off as a regular afternoon smoke session didn't end as one. A couple of other officers joined this session and I was zeroed in on. Three officers were yelling different things at me, while I was made to stand in the middle of the floor holding a long dumb bell or a sort of joust stick. It was heavy and I had to squat with it for about an hour. All while they were still yelling at me, I guess to break me down. That was not it, then I had to go to the office and that's when it all came out. One officer said, "You from New York?", then she started asking me if I was from the hood and if I was a hood rat? It was so crazy she went so far as to call me a "B" also known as a female dog. Angry was too mild a word for how I felt. After a while I just did not respond. I shut my mouth even when asked a question, and one tear after another began to slowly roll down my face.

To me all of that was not necessary to build a person into a soldier. Do not break a person's spirit down and then expect them to be happy you built them back up a supposedly better way. While a person's being rebuilt, that break down is going to be on their mind and they will resent you for it. Not long after that I decided I just wanted "out" so I stopped speaking to my Petty Officers and superiors. They made me stand under the stairs in my ship, which was really a building. A lot of other military personnel would walk by this stairway. So it was like open season, when they saw me sitting under the stairs. They would laugh and tell me to stand up so they could yell at me and grill me on what I did to be there. They must have thought I was insane because I would just look at them and not respond.

Then I was sent to a psychiatrist for an evaluation. I told her I was wetting the bed and was not sleeping at night. I began to tell her my niece had died and I was worried about my family including my mother who was on drugs. Yes, it became one lie after another. My sister did fall and she had a miscarriage before, but I was not troubled by it. My mother was not on drugs anymore (I think), bed wetting was not a problem for me anymore since I was a child, and sleeping at night was just upsetting to me because it was very cold on those barracks with a thin jail like blanket. At the end of all of those lies I was finally discharged from my 478 shipmates, sent to another set of barracks with a group of people that were leaving too. Then off to my new home in a new state. Being that I could not face the questions everyone would ask me if I returned home from the Navy early, Atlanta Georgia seemed like the best place to hide and get away from having to answer those questions.

East Point, Georgia close to Washington road was where I ended up and lived with my boyfriend Walter and his college friends. I had been to Atlanta several times when I was in high school but living there was so much different. I was not able to go back home to see and visit my friends and family when the weekend was over with. Yes, I began to get homesick again. On one hand I wanted to be starting a life in a new place. On the other hand I was not ready to let go of all the familiar things I knew and grew up around. This made my life in Atlanta miserable. Partying, drinking and smoking were not things I was originally into doing. However all of the people I was around were partying, drinking and smoking. My boyfriend, his roommate and all of the people he knew (seven) were doing it. Later I began to hang with this one girl from Detroit. Everyone called her "Red". Before she left Atlanta to go

back home, I was in desperate need for my own apartment.
One night we went to visit one of her friends. She just
so happen to also be searching for a roommate. Red had
advised me not to move in with the girl but she refused to
tell me why. So being that I did not have a valid reason not
to move in with her I moved in. Living with her and being
on my own was great; at first.

Her and my boyfriend began arguing a lot, sort
of like a couple would. This caused me to question what
previous relationship they had before I moved to Atlanta.
As I began my inquiries he was adamant that nothing was
going on nor had anything ever in the past went on with
them. My heart just did not believe him. Then it happened
he finally broke and said well she use to like me. This
really meant there was a lot more to this story. By the end
of a long and exhausting question and answer game, he
stated they spoke on the phone a few times but never were
intimately involved. Yeah right! There was more to the
story, but I just did not have the energy to find out anymore
of his hidden secrets. The reason I knew something went
on between them was because this was not the first time
he confessed (halfway) about a female he had either been
intimately involved with or was close to being intimate with.
Yes, I can finally admit that he was a cheater and definitely
a liar. When I felt an inch of love, I naively began to accept
a mile of crap. Yeah, I felt hurt and betrayed but even then
I wanted to believe the best about the guy I thought I loved.
More so, I did not want to lose the little love I was getting
from him.

I spoke with Red about the issues in the apartment
and her response was, "I told you not to move in with her".
So I simply reminded her she did not give me any reason
not to. Well come to find out she knew about whatever

went on between them. In my mind I was the only dummy that did not know. To top it all off, I was now pregnant and even more emotional than normal. Eventually I started staying back at my boyfriend's place more and more because I was very uncomfortable being around my boyfriend and roommate in the same place. Then when I decided to move out I went to pick up my things and to my surprise the locks were changed. I was furious and in disbelief. First of all, she was in the wrong. Secondly, she acted like I was a thief or some ghetto hood chick. Well my Brooklyn boyfriend got us in the apartment and I definitely retrieved my belongings. Needless to say we did not speak after that. In the end, I felt bad about how everything played out between us. I was just really hurt after discovering they had something going on. Whether it was in the past or at the time I was not certain. After Red left Atlanta the only person I hung out with was my roommate.

Why couldn't I have a roommate that did not like my boyfriend? Now I'm back to living in this crowded and filthy apartment with these nasty guys. The more pregnant I became, the more my boyfriend partied and left me there alone. I would just cry and cry and ask myself why am I even here? We started arguing all of the time about him leaving me in the apartment with nothing to do while he lived a fun filled life of drugs and alcohol. Now how stupid was that? I desired to be on drugs and drink alcohol. Yes weed, marijuana, trees however you prefer it to be labeled it was and still is a drug.

This one night I was about five months pregnant and he was going to the club again. We started arguing before he got ready to leave and he pushed me very forcefully onto the bed and then climbed on top of me to hold my arms down and yell in my face. It became crazy. Things just seemed like they were going from bad to worse, to extremely worst. He did the whole apology thing and then still he continued on and left for the club. Oh what a night that turned out to be…the beginning of my new found abusive relationship. He grabbed and held me down a few more times after that. I surprised him one day when he thought he was going to push me around. He charged at me and I quickly grabbed a big kitchen knife. Superman chose to keep coming towards a whaling sharp object. He should not have been surprised or angry about obtaining a huge forearm laceration. My intentions were to scare him into backing up and not getting physical. It did not quite play out like I imagined.

He decided to join the military a few weeks earlier. Now his decision was sealed or should I say stitched. It was conveniently revealed to me when I was driving him to the prepaid military assigned hotel that we should break up. Tears were coming down my eyes like buckets of water. I am thinking this must be a joke. He could not really be breaking up with me after getting me pregnant, making me have to move out of my apartment, asking me to move to another state and now right before he leaves he is breaking up with me. He was such a jerk but we got back together. He probably felt pity for me and blurted out, "Ok let's stay together", just to stop me from crying.

I know I was young and dumb and in need of any kind of love. So it was no surprise when I had the baby and he came home for the visit that I found letters from another girl in his bag. They had been together for the past four or five months and she was saying how much she loved him and how much fun she's been having with him. It was a disgusting feeling inside my stomach that I was all too familiar with. After we had that long battle he finally admitted he was seeing her and they had been intimate. I told him of how he was a lying, cheating bastard and then he was gone.

He spent that 1999 thanksgiving with her in Virginia and I was in Atlanta with my new baby boy Jahlil. I convinced my sister Nisha to move to Atlanta with her boyfriend and their son. Living in New York was okay but it was not the best place to raise a family, at least not where we grew up. The amazing part about Nisha moving was that she somehow convinced Kizzy to move here too. I never thought Kizzy would ever leave the father of her children or Brooklyn, but she did.

After they were living in Atlanta, Kizzy and I went to New York that Christmas with our new baby boys. Walter was in New York with his new girlfriend and her family. It was so crazy now that I think about it; we would talk on the phone while he was at her house. "That's not my girlfriend" was his favorite lie. How could he say they might get married if she was not his girlfriend? It was drama after drama. We exchanged unpleasant words over the telephone a couple of times and then there were the phone calls from my friends late at night that began occurring to her home. He had the nerve to tell me he was torn between living his single life of attending night clubs verses being committed to our longtime relationship. On top of that we were now parents and he was scared of ruining our child's life. Being torn was not his dilemma, being a selfish coward was his problem. The both of them went back to the Army base and I stayed in New York. We still talked on a regular basis. He would tell me of when he and his girlfriend went to play pool and we even discussed their sex life. We talked about when they went to the movies and he compared it to when we would sneak in and watch an extra movie at the theatre. His constant complaint was that she was not like me and he missed me. Last time I checked he cheated on me and he made the decision to start a relationship with her.

Then one cold January night he called me to say
he was ready to be with me and leave this other girl alone.
My first question was why? She started pressuring him
to get married and he initially wanted a break from our
relationship to live life and now he is ready to start being a
family with me and Jahlil. There were trust issues between
us, but he was the father of my son and I thought I was not
ready to raise a child alone at twenty years old. By March
he asked me to move to North Carolina to be with him.
We planned on starting a real family so by April we were
literally married with a child. He placed my finger inside
his mouth and between his teeth was my engagement
ring. He asked me to marry him and these emotions were
not what I anticipated on having. It was a sweet proposal
but instead of joy taking my breath away, my stomach was
doing flips of doubt. I thought I loved him and I thought
I forgave him. Maybe I was not ready for marriage even if
I told him I wanted to be married. Fear held me back that
proposal night and then again at the court house. The fear
of losing him because I did not want to get married and
having to be alone was not a situation I was prepared for. It
just did not feel like the correct choice but I did it anyway. I
was the coward now because I could not express to him my
reservations about us getting married.

After the court house wedding, a desire to know
God began to brew inside me. I enrolled in a fork lifting
class at the local college where I met this Muslim man. He
began to tell me Jesus was simply another prophet, not
God like Christians believed along with some other stuff I
forgot. I was invited to the Masjid with him and his wife.
The experience was not memorable but his confidence
and knowledge was convincing to me. That was my last
visit with them to the Masjid. A Quran and their contact
information were given to me as I began my journey to

pursue "God". I went to a different Masjid a few times
after that but failed to fully commit my life. I went to a
few Arabic language classes as well. This was encouraged
in order to get the full understanding of the Quran which
was translated from its original Arabic language. During
any translation the exact meaning is at times lost due to a
translator's interpretation of each word. Or in some cases
the lack of a specific word from one language to another can
cause an unintentional error. Although that was new and
interesting, between raising a baby and my new marriage I
had zero time for learning about this new god or language.
I claimed to be Muslim because I believed what I heard but
I wasn't a practicing Muslim in the sense.

With my young husband being in the military I
noticed him changing for the worst. I do not agree that the
military makes people crazy. It just brings out what was
already inside of a person. We argued every day and for
the most frivolous things. Making up was a popular event
in our house. The arguments turned into him grabbing
me and pushing me. Afterwards the slap came here and
there, followed by deep apologies. Then a slap turned into
a punch, which for some odd reason was followed by fewer
apologies. You would think after being slapped around and
having a busted lip I would leave. Maybe I was blind or just
flat out stupid because I stayed and endured more.

One time I thought he was actually going to kill me.
We argued for whatever reason. I was fed up with being his
punching bag so for the first time I hit him back. Oh how
that set him off, he hit me so hard after that I almost fell
to the living room floor. It continued with the usual name
calling, slapping and pushing to the ground. This escalated
to him grabbing me by the hair and pulling some out. He
gathered some saliva in his mouth and then spat it directly

into my face. At that point I was empty within myself. For a man to spit in your face he had to think really lowly of you. And I unmistakably had to think lowly of myself to allow such an act. That was not it, he then began choking me to the point I felt like I was going to pass out. As my ten month old son watched in horror, I heard his screams and saw his tears. I owed it to my son to beg for my life. After a few more hits and my screams for help it was finally over. Jahlil was red from crying and I could only hold him in my arms as my mind replayed this traumatic event. What did I get myself into? Was this the same fifteen year old that held my hand and held me as my painful past arose? No way could this be the same person that waited a year before we were intimate and then went out and brought breakfast prior to me waking up. I never thought this man would ever transform into this monster I have come to know and hate.

Another time he tried to block my car in with his and when I was exiting I hit his car. As I got out, checking the damage I noticed him driving towards me. I jumped back in the car and before I could shut the door he smashed my door in. I drove away with a door that could not completely close. I believe I called the police and somehow I was arrested for assault with a deadly weapon. With his military status he seemed to be untouchable. He would hit me and when I called the police he would say I hit him followed by saying he's in the military. They would tell him to go cool off then they would leave. So much for protecting and serving!

I started to work as a security guard and take all the hours I could get. Saving money for my own place and a new car was my goal. This guy at my job became interested in me or should I say we became interested in one another's bodies? We did not take the relationship far. It was a way to escape my inward pain. I actually thought I was worthless. My heart was bursting with pain and anger, yet at the same time yearning for a touch of peace. A peace I chased but could never catch. Torment was how I lived in my mind day in and day out. My situation was made worse by me. For me to constantly relive the pain of abandonment from my mother and the abuse by this man it was no wonder I became depressed. By the time I decided to move back to Atlanta I had been arrested for assault with a deadly weapon, more assaults charges and ordered to attend anger management.

A month before I left North Carolina he moved in with one of his soldier friends. As I was on the way to our anger management class I saw him driving the opposite direction with a female in the car. I made a U-turn and followed him which led to a high speed chase for over ten minutes then it hit me, I was crazy too. What was I doing chasing him? If he wanted to sleep around with other woman that was on him, I needed to focus on me at this point. The anger management classes allowed me to see I was in an abusive relationship and I was headed for death or murder. For me to not have known that before they told me was absolute denial on my part. Death or murder neither sounded like my childhood aspirations so I called Stacy from the Group Home and just cried out to her and told her everything that had been happening between us. She calmly told me to pray and eat something. I informed her I had not eaten in about two days and was just depressed and ready to change. I did not know how to pray so I just cried and said God why is this happening to me? Why can't I just be happy? Why can't I just be loved? Why did he do this to me? Why didn't he love me anymore? What did I do that was so wrong he had to hit me? Why didn't my mother

want me? Why wasn't I good enough for her? All of this
came out and I just released it and cried my heart and hurt
out. I ate some soup, gave away most of my furniture,
let him take some items and I packed up my car and son
and headed back to Atlanta. This experience changed me
mentally. I was unsure about life and love. My identity
was unknown and I was empty within myself. Although
I wanted to make better decisions for my future I did not
know how. I was consumed with self-hatred and my pity
enabled me to make excuses for my actions. Thank God I
came into the knowledge that was not real love.

        I returned to Atlanta in late 2000, my sisters Kizzy
and Nisha were living in my old apartment with their
children and now we were all in a small two bedroom
apartment together. Shortly after, either this man was very
persuasive or I was very ignorant. I went back to North
Carolina initially to handle a "medical situation" and then
we presumed marital relations. After one or two months
I went back home to Atlanta and started working at the
airport, which only lasted a month. My arrest in North
Carolina came back on my criminal background check and
just like that I was fired. Kizzy and I decided to move into
a bigger two bedroom apartment. Although I did not have
a job my distant spouse sent me rent money. I also braided
hair and participated in stealing clothes for extra income.

        Thanks to my overextended visit out of state I was
now three months pregnant. This was supposed to be our
final breakup so the suggestion of abortion came up and I
was not fond of that idea. I agreed verbally, but my heart
was not into crossing that rocky bridge again I tried to bury
in the past. He sent me the money for the abortion clinic
but did not send the monthly rent money. So I decided
to not get the abortion with the money and pay the rent

instead. Throughout the pregnancy I traveled back and
forth to North Carolina. Pregnant and the day before my
birthday, on September 11, as I watched television I saw
an airplane crash into the New York twin towers. The
entire day my eyes were glued to the news channel, which
happened to be on every channel that day. Many lives were
lost and affected by the terrorist attacks that occurred that
sad day in America.

By October I was back in Atlanta and awaiting my
second child. While I was cleaning my bedroom around
one o'clock in the morning I began to have slight stomach
pains, so I decided to take a shower. As I sat in the tub with
the shower running onto my stomach I felt the baby coming
out. I woke up my sister Kizzy for assistance because now
I could barely walk and I strongly desired to push this baby
out. She called 911 for an ambulance as I laid on the edge
of my bed with my legs open. As I was restraining myself
from pushing the Fire Department arrived. The female
fire fighter had the pleasure of delivering my new baby girl
that late October morning in 2001. Tears of joy fell down
my face as I held my new baby I named Jillian. Tragically
my four year old cousin in New York died after surgery this
same day.

Being a mother of two small children and having
a broken marriage, I had no idea who I really was. Two
months later in December of 2001 Brooklyn, New York was
my next stop.

Chapter 4
Whirlwind Years

*F*inally after a long year in New York I returned back to Atlanta again. It seemed as though I was drawn there. With Jahlil, Jillian and my husband, and our marriage hanging on by a string we wanted to make our marriage work. My plan was to go back to Atlanta because the steps I was making in New York just kept leading to dead ends. So we went to my apartment I shared with my sister Kizzy and her two children. My mother and younger sister Princess were staying at the apartment in the living room when I first left. I thought it was amazing for Kizzy moving to

Atlanta but when my mother moved here that was a flat out miracle! A crowded apartment was better than residing in different New York shelters with two small children.

Every night I would have to sign into this one shelter by ten p.m. if I remember correctly and on Friday I would sign out for the entire weekend. I signed out on Friday night so I could get away and go to my grandmother's house until Sunday. One weekend I forgot to sign out for all three days, so when I got back I was discharged and we had to leave. A girlfriend of mine was in a battered woman's shelter and told me that I could get housing quicker if I signed into one too. Initially I was hesitant because I had been to domestic abuse counseling and I just did not want to be questioned or reliving those events.

Then push came to shove I checked into a battered women's shelter. I was enrolled in a downtown Brooklyn computer training school with one of the girls from the group home. She attended for A+ certification and I was interested in computer hardware repairs. In one of my classes I met this older gentleman who traveled the globe and knew more about computers than the teachers. There were four of us that cliqued up at school. Larry was about fifty and had a twenty something year old girlfriend. We studied, discussed bigger aspirations than this small fast paced New York City life, he also fried tilapia fish fillets and we smoked joints of marijuana. He made me believe my vision of residing in a huge home with a happy family was possible. With him being successful by having multiple properties and great business plans, it had to be possible for me.

I took the bus and train daily to drop off my children next door from their father's place to their grandfather's house so he could babysit while I took another train to school. It was a lot especially when I decided to check into the domestic violence shelter. The shelter was in Harlem away from everything I was familiar with. There was a bright side. I was accepted to the Manhattan location for the computer school I attended. The commute was shorter and the shelter provided childcare while I went to school. While going to school I found a Masjid a couple of blocks away. I visited a few times, but I questioned the need for women to pray behind the men or in a separate room. Other than that I believed what I was taught by the fellow Muslims. When I left the Masjid I was no longer around Muslims, so I did not have the opportunity to grow stronger spiritually. My religious status was still that of a Muslim even though I was very spiritually and knowledgably weak. What I knew was Jesus was a man and I was not going to follow a man like those ignorant Christians did.

Being that domestic violence was a very dangerous situation for these women, their children and I the location was not to be disclosed to anyone. Prior to moving into the shelter I applied for a school safety officer position. This was my opportunity to obtain a stable and good paying job. I was scheduled to take the physical but I had to be there around 7am, which meant I had to leave by 5am to travel to Queens. Now the problem was the shelter rules stated that I could not leave that early. Unless I put in a special request, which I did the day before I had to take the exam. No, I was not procrastinating. All of my mail was delivered to my children's grandmother's house. By the time she gave it to me it was just about time to take the exam. Another great opportunity down the drain, it seemed as if when one door opened two doors and a window closed on me.

The children were invited to spend the day with their grandparents at the Brooklyn Coney Island theme park. After a great day of food, fun and rides they requested we meet at the train station to pick up the children. Somehow we missed each other, while I was at the train station Jahlil told them he needed to use the bathroom so his grandfather took him to the shelter to use the bathroom. My son was smart and had a good sense of direction so he walked his grandfather there. Needless to say due to the strict confidentiality of the shelter's location we were discharged and had to leave yet again. By this time I was fed up and frustrated because nothing I was doing seemed to be working.

I guess my children's grandmother felt sorry for me so I began staying with her. When I moved in, my on and off again husband began coming by a lot more. One night as I was getting ready to go visit my friend from computer school he decided to get jealous and inquire where I was going all dressed up and smelling good. So being that we were not even together and he had been messing around with a few girls he assumed I was involved with my friend. An older man was not what I desired. We were smoking buddies and his girlfriend was mostly always there, which Mr. Jealous already knew. So I continued getting ready and he began following me around the apartment questioning me. His mother and our children were in the apartment the entire time. After he lost it in his mind he decided to lose it on my face.

He punched me in the face and naturally busted my lip. Although he had hit me before it was never in the presence of anyone. I called the police. He left and his mother was crying and asked me not to call my family to beat up her son. The whole time I'm thinking all you can think about is your abusive son and I'm the one always getting my face bashed in. The police came and I told them I couldn't press charges because I was staying at his mother's house and I really did not have anywhere else to go. I still made my way over to visit my friend, I told him what happened and we just sat around smoking weed and talking about our rich futures. After that night I decided to leave New York and head back to Atlanta with only my children. Right before I was about to leave Walter and I had a long talk about trying to make our marriage work and how he wouldn't lose control like that anymore. So being gullible I fell for it in a way. I said, "Let's make it work", but in my mind I vowed if he so much as pushed me I was leaving for good. My mind was so made up that when we finally got our own place together in Atlanta I put all the bills and apartment in my name only.

Prior to obtaining a security job I went back to braiding hair, selling boosted (stolen) clothes and returning boosted or selling electronics for cash or store credit. In a short time I had new furniture, electronics and all the clothes I wanted for me and my children. I had so much stuff that I had to get a storage unit to hold everything. Braiding hair was more like a creative hobby, it definitely wasn't a passion. At this point in my life stealing was my passion.

We would go into department stores dressed in very nice attire like a dress, no jeans or sneakers and not in a large group. Most of the time one person would pick out maybe ten expensive dresses, take then to the fitting room and remove the alarm devices. If I was that person I usually had a baby in a stroller so after I removed the alarms I placed them in a baby diaper then threw it in the cashiers trash can. Or if I had a fast food bag I placed the alarms in there then threw that bag in the cashiers trash can. These dresses ranged from a hundred and fifty dollars to four hundred and fifty dollars. When the alarms were off the second person came into the dressing room to fold the dresses and then placed them on the bottom of their baby stroller. The two people pretended not to know each other and we moved very quickly. We did this about three days a week, not counting our smaller personal thefts.

Another method was to buy men's clothing with a department store credit card. This way allowed the usually hard alarms to be removed legally and provided us with a receipt. Before the purchase was made we had to have two identical garments of whatever was to be bought and we needed a new looking department store bag that we came into the store with. One person picked out double garments, purchased one set and left the second set in a specified location. The next person with the department store bag that was brought in placed the second set of garments into their bag with the alarms still in tack while the other person was purchasing. When the purchase was complete and the second bag was loaded, the receipt was swiftly and nonchalantly passed to the other person. By doing this the person with the security alarms still in tack would proceed out the department store and the alarm would go off. When security would check the bag and see the alarms still on they then asked for the receipt, which we had. They assumed the cashier forgot to take off the alarm and the first person was walking out the store in the clear. The second person now had to take the merchandise and the receipt back to a cashier to be removed. This usually took about fifteen minutes in total to complete. The next day or two we would return one set of merchandise and we sold or gave away the second set. In a week's time we did this over ten times. We typically did this procedure when we needed a requested outfit to sell someone, if we had a personal want or if we were getting holiday gifts.

Now when it came to stealing electronics I had a high Marijuana never gave me. The thrill was extremely huge. We went to well-known supercenters that carried food, clothes and electronics. In the beginning we stole things we needed, but could not afford like seasoning, baby formula, medicine and meat. Then when we needed bigger items that could not fit in our bags we decided to take a small but expensive item that we would return for store credit.

As time went on we would walk in with fake return items to get the return stickers. With these stickers we were able to return whatever we wanted. This led to high end electronics like televisions and computers. After we got the stickers we would go shopping instead of returning the item. We located our new item placed the sticker on that and then go to the return counter. We returned the new item like a television and purchased our groceries all at the same time.

Eventually we used one of our department store methods to steal the electronics. We would purchase computers, televisions, printers, DVD players and all the accessories we obtained a receipt and gave it to the next person. The second person went in with the receipt picked up the same item after matching the receipt numbers to the merchandise then successfully exited the store. This went on in the same day until the cars were filled or the door attendant placed a big yellow check mark on the receipt. Of course the first item was returned for our cash.

I alone gave about five computers away and had one of my own. There were about four other main players plus the people we sometimes used to help. The main players had their own computers and they gave or sold about four

Chapter 4 WHIRLWIND YEARS

or more themselves. The recruits were paid with computers, televisions or gift cards. Those were not the only items. We also stole vacuums, DVD movies, cameras, pots, bikes, blenders, toys, scanners, picture frames, chairs, microwaves, toasters, bedding, and the list goes on and on. Other players became so bold that they stole the door attendant's roll of return stickers. It was a great business. Whatever we wanted materially, we had. Getting caught was not my focus. I thought I was cleverer than the store security team. Most of the time I went in the morning whenever I was alone because it seemed to me the security surveillance was low during that time.

When I was twelve I began stealing food and miscellaneous items, then at fifteen clothes were added to my list which I continued to do until 2005. Throughout the years I have had family members and friends accompany me on these adventures and I was caught about five times in thirteen years. Out of those five times I was caught during my teenage years. I was caught prior to me mastering my craft. Here is the bonus, I was never arrested and I did not have a shoplifting record. I knew plenty of people that did get arrested and I purposed myself not to go stealing with them. They did not know when to be patient long enough to observe the area for undercover security. Three out of the five times I was caught, I was with someone else who either began looking like they were stealing or who got scared and made a mistake meanwhile every time I knew something was wrong. Listening to your body's instincts was imperative to a successful stealing career. It was a learned skill that I enjoyed and became rather good at. Being a thief was not how I planned to live my entire life especially having two children to raise. The security job was a big step towards a normal life, but it did not pay enough for me to quit stealing. Stealing was an addiction in a sense so at that time I could have probably been making a good amount of honest money and it would not have mattered.

The other parts of my life were also spiraling like a whirlwind. Although my husband and I did not get physical while at the shared apartment with my mother, two sisters and four small children, he kicked in the front door and threw the cordless phone clear across the street. Needless to say it broke into pieces and was unusable. This was becoming embarrassing and now everyone was going to know I was with a lunatic. We moved out after that and stayed with his family.

Then we finally moved into our own apartment, I believe he waited until he had me alone before exploding back to his old self. Yes it happened after a few months of no physical incidents we got into an argument and he pushed me. I fell backwards and busted the bedroom wall and he nonchalantly walked away and got into the shower. I remembered my vow and I immediately went downstairs called East Point city police to remove him from the apartment. After the police officers asked him to get out the shower all I heard was a loud commotion and I looked in the room and they had him naked on the floor. One Officer punched him in the face and the other one kicked or stomped on his back. Later the officer that punched him stated he punched him because he bit his leg. They took him out the apartment and placed him in the police car. A minute later he kicked out the police car window and the officer sprayed him with mace. It was a crazy situation for us all. I have never liked violence so to see him get beat up and mace did not make me feel vengeance in any way. Or could it be that abused people have mixed feelings? On one hand you desire your abuser to know the pain and suffering they are putting you through. Then on the other hand you love that person so much and could not stand to see anything harmful happen to them. The answer to the big question about why does a woman stay with a man that abuses her? It is clear because the mind of a victim is as twisted as the mind of the abuser.

Some people would argue fear of being killed by their abuser or fear of having to start life all over again after years of being taken care of. Maybe that was true in some instances, but the bottom line was a twisted mindset. We separated after that incident and he began staying on my mother's couch. If that sounds weird to you, imagine how weird it sounded to me. She would call me and complain how lazy and sloppy he was and my response would always be well you let him stay, so now that's your problem. He then moved into his cousin's apartment nearby and occasionally threw rocks at my window as an attempt to get a conversation going in order to get in my apartment. He never made it in but I visited him at his place. It took a very long time but I was not going to tolerate his abusive ways anymore. Although we never officially reunited, we did engage in intimate activity after our separation until late 2004.

After being a security officer for a few years off and on, I decided to make a career move. I was ready to act like an adult with a career and of course that good old American dream. My desire was for that white house with a picket fence and a pretty dog. I had a nice green tinted window station wagon that looked brand new, I had Jahlil and Jillian and hey I even had a husband I was getting ready to finally divorce. So now all I really needed I felt was the dream job. I was working at a place called Underground Atlanta as a security guard and I was not going to let that be the end of the road for me. I met a police officer who brought me an application to fill out to become a policeman. He even threw in a bit of doubt that I would not complete it, so of course that pushed me to expeditiously turn in the application.

Making this new career move meant I would have to give up smoking marijuana and stealing, which I decided to do. The following week the application was turned in. When I was in high school I wanted to be a police officer, but my grandmother did not think that would be a good idea so I did not do it. Grandma was not here now! After passing a physical, drug screen, psyche test and a criminal background check I was a police recruit. Meaning I was on the waiting list to attend the police academy as soon as enough recruits for a class were enlisted. In the meantime I was placed at police headquarters to basically do errand work with pay of course. Then the news came in that my divorce was final. I was so happy to be moving on with my new life I cried tears of joy. My mind set had been to start a new life full of love and no regrets. I was so focused on getting through the academy I hardly spoke to anyone at work. Another recruit that everyone said looked like me from Detroit asked me to walk with her to get a smoothie. While we were walking she told me more great news that we were getting ready to leave for the academy. That was the icing on my cake. I was so happy I told her what a great day I was having because today was also the day my divorce was final. She was happy for me and probably a bit shocked that this girl who had been so quiet was expressing such personal information.

The first day at the academy started so wrong. I had no clue how to get to the academy and all the other police recruits had left police headquarters already. Thankfully I knew a girl that worked in central records and she introduced me to this officer who worked at the academy but was on administrative duty due to a sex scandal involving him and a few other officers that worked with him. He quickly gave me directions and I sped out of there so fast his head spun.

I knew I could not be late and I definitely was not going to be the one to stand out. This was a subject I was all too familiar with and I knew the "dos and don'ts". Do what they say and don't do anything stupid, that simple. A lesson learned from my time in naval boot camp in 1998. After I sweated in my clothes with fear of being late, I made it in time for formation which was in alphabetical order.

We were all standing in line without obvious verbal communication. Then people began to wonder what we were waiting for. They soon found out after a bonehead male recruit went and knocked on the door to inform the academy we arrived. When he got back in line formation, officers busted out of all the doors charging and screaming at us to do pushups, asking us questions with spit flying in our faces, screaming at the bonehead asking him why he knocked on the door. Then they made us run into the gymnasium where they called us up one by one to take a close look at us and ask us questions. More like insults in question form, but there was not any right answer they were looking for. They were just searching for fear and weakness to latch onto so they could get rid of it or that person. It was so funny to me because I had already been through this type of pressure. This situation was not so funny to this one guy in particular. He was so scared he began crying and he was not able to follow the multiple commands from the officers. They were asking him questions while he was doing squats, jumping jacks and pushups. By the time they were finished with him, he was crying. The question to ask yourself if you don't agree with their method is "Would I want this crying person helping me in a drug deal arrest that has turned into a fight for my life?" The answer is probably not.

The training consisted of a lot of running. Muscle rub became my best friend for the pain. My New York attitude and demeanor showed on my face, which did not make me a popular recruit in a good way. I got in trouble for anything it seemed, but thankfully the female recruit from Detroit also known as my twin looked like me to them too. We began sharing my punishment not willingly or happily on her part. During a defensive training exercise everyone had to have a partner place their hands around the other person's neck while sitting on top of the other person as to demonstrate a frontal choke hold on the ground. As my male partner sat on top of me as soon as he placed his hands around my neck my mind flashed back to that North Carolina night and I stopped him. He asked if I was okay then attempted to try the tactic again. This time my eyes began to fill up with tears and I felt as though I could not fully breathe. My friend from Detroit switched places with him, but I could not hold myself together. She escorted me to the bathroom and tears just came pouring out. I had no idea this encounter was instilled in my heart to this extent. Focusing was very crucial at this point. I vaguely explained what was occurring with me when we headed back out. With teary eyes and a constricting airway we completed the exercise successfully.

A big mouthed male recruit that occasionally flirted with me made a comment about me sleeping with another recruit. This was serious because if his comment made its way to the instructional officers and they believed him I could have been fired. After an intense workout for getting in trouble, three of us were in the lunch room area when the comment was made towards me again. We then exchanged unpleasant words. A female recruit came between us to settle down the confrontation and told him to be quiet. We were not allowed to talk to each other so as another male

recruit came into the lunch area he told her to be quiet
before we got into trouble again. This led to them arguing
and ultimately they shoved each other and then in came
our instructor. The two recruits were discharged and upon
investigation they told about the alleged involvement of me
and another person made by the big mouthed recruit. We
both denied it and now two other people were out of a job.
I felt responsible for a while and she blamed me too. It put
a huge strain on our friendship. Both recruits were allowed
to obtain recruitment status in a later class and it just so
happened they were in the same class again. We finally
graduated and I was assigned to morning watch.

One night at home as I was smoking a blunt, I began
watching a movie that began to change my thinking. This
boy had been sold into slavery by his own brothers because
they were jealous of his relationship with their father. This
young man became a slave. Then he was put in jail for
allegedly attempting to rape his master's wife. While in jail
he became the second man in charge of Egypt. He was over
all the people he was once in slaved to and abused by. He
never thought about getting them back for all the wrong
they did to him in the past. The best part was when his very
own brothers came to him in need of food to survive. He
forgave them and continued to love them in spite of what
they did to him. He did not remind them of the wrong
they committed against him. My heart was so heavy with
a deficiency of forgiveness towards people in my life that
I broke down into tears. I searched for that movie every
chance I could, to watch it again. At the time I had no idea
it was one of the events in the bible. A few times after the
movie I watched church services on television but I desired
more practical information in a way I could understand. I
thought that God was real but thinking that was not enough
for me anymore. Having a relationship with my God and

changing my thinking was what I was after. I could not
seem to find that relationship I was after and in many ways I
was scared to make that change of lifestyle.

In late 2004, when I was driving down the street on
the way to a criminal trespass 911 call my patrol car flipped
over and smashed into an electrical pole (or it could have
hit the pole then flipped over). I was in a bit of shock at
first. One minute I was driving, the next I was upside down
in the car. I radioed the dispatch operator for help and then
I remember this man asking me was I alright. My seatbelt
was not on, the windows were all busted out and the electric
wires were live on top of the car. Then the man assisted me
in crawling out of the driver side window. He warned me
to be careful because of the wires. Then he said, "You are
lucky to be alive." I tried to act like everything was okay so
I took my police bag out the car and placed it on the ground
and waited for the responding officers. The sounds of their
sirens were in the background as I analyzed the overturned
car I could have died in.

Another bystander or two came to make sure
everything was alright with me. Somewhere between the
arrival of the officers and the ambulance, the man that
helped me out of the car was gone and so was my police
bag. I could not give a complete description of the man that
helped me, nor could I say where my bag went. Actually it
really did not matter to me. My mind and heart wondered
why I didn't die, I wanted to be dead. I did not have any
body aches afterward. I did have a tiny scratch on my cheek
from a piece of glass. Other than that, I did not have any
physical evidence of the accident. It was so tiny no one
noticed it, but me. An officer friend of mine said God must
have something for you to do (or something along those
lines). That statement made my yearning for God grow

even stronger. For about a month after that I just wondered why my life was speared. What was my purpose in life? Was this the career for me? Was this the state for me? It seemed like more questions came to me than answers.

I continued to smoke weed and when my high would start to come down I would jump back into smoking a blunt or drinking a shot of whatever alcohol I had in my house. Feelings of being unfulfilled, alone, unloved, unworthy of being a good mother, being a bad police officer and just not being where I thought I should be in life began to pound inside my head. I was in a home I loved and I had a car loaded with a TV, DVD player, a new sound system and tinted windows. I already had the children and I had a police officer I was sleeping with. With all of that, I was still empty inside. I was not fulfilled within myself or with myself. There were a few nights I tried to end my sorrows but I never followed through with completing it. The last attempt, I was high on marijuana, placed my grey 40 caliber gun in my mouth and then shoved it into my abdomen thankfully without success.

Being that I did not make the two children I was raising alone on my own, anger kicked in towards the man that lived less than three minutes up the street from us with a woman and her daughter. He was in adultery with this woman when we were still married. All I asked of him was to help out with keeping the children at night while I worked, simple enough right? Well not for him. He occasionally gave our children money and hardly spent time with them. I could not understand how he could turn around and borrow money from me and quite often, more baffling was how I could be so stupid to lend him money. Then after a month of keeping them at night and coming late at times while I worked, he said he could not do it

anymore. I was so fed up with him, with my job schedule
and the lack of childcare. I told him that he would have to
keep the children because that was not fair for me to do his
part and mine. He agreed because he did not want to pay
child support that he rarely paid anyway. I was missing
so many days at work and not really caring about the job
because of the lack of child care support I had at home for
my young children. My request for a day shift was denied at
work then I began putting in daily requests and just getting
more and more frustrated with the police department.
After we had a few discussions I sent my children to live
with him.

After Jahlil and Jillian were gone my smoking and
drinking increased so much I never let myself come down
from being high. I grew stronger in my anger for their
father and the police department. They both pushed me
into a corner to have to give up my children, I thought.
At the time that was the only road I saw and in my mind
it would all change in a year at the most. Then I became
infuriated because why wasn't there any help for me? I just
wanted to provide for my children the things I never had
and help people in a position many viewed as authoritative.
When in actuality, at times being a police officer was to
perform the opposite of help. As police officers we should
not dictate to the people, we are there to serve. Often
times with us having so much power with our badges, we
tend to become rude, uncompassionate and extremely
aggressive and hostile towards everyone. When in fact we
are supposed to be there to help, protect and serve. I knew I
was there to help, comfort and then protect the people. My
main focus was not to just simply arrest or give someone
a traffic summons but that is what the job advises you to
focus on.

After being on a downward binge I was invited to
church by Walter. My response was laughter at first then I
said yeah simply because I did not want him to think he had
me down. I wanted to remind him of what he was missing
with me and also I was high. When I awoke the next
morning to go to church I quickly realized I did not want
to go. So in order to get myself to go I rolled another blunt,
smoked half of it and then got dressed. I put on one of my
normal cute outfits: shoe boots, tight pants, a nice beige hat
and of course a pair of dark sunglasses. Then I was ready to
go.

Chapter 5
Un-natural Birth

*T*his un-natural birth was not of a child but it was that of a twenty-five year old woman with two children. Growing up I never imagined my life past the age of twenty-five. I always thought I would die in some way and eventually I did. This death did not happen the ways in which I imagined. While I was driving north on Interstate 85 to Buckhead smoking what was left of my morning blunt I realized I left the directions Walter gave me to the church at home. Even though I was high, I still remembered some of the directions after a wrong turn. I found the church and it looked like an office building. Sunday, April 17th, 2005 at 12:00 pm I made my presence known at a church service that would change my life, as I knew it.

It was as though this preacher began speaking directly to me without making direct eye contact with me. He discussed smoking marijuana, drinking alcohol, not being whole, sex before marriage and tattoos. There were other subjects discussed that I really cannot remember because I was so high from smoking marijuana before church. All of the activities I was currently partaking in. A week earlier I added two more tattoos to my body. One tattoo I got put on my lower mid back and another on my lower right stomach area. At church I remember thinking, is this real? At the end of service another man came up to speak and he asked did anyone need to come to the front to be saved. I had no idea what that actually meant but I knew I should be up there. A new life with God had to be much greater than the life I had now. However deep down I was afraid and began to make excuses why I should not go up to the front. I was high on drugs and felt ashamed to go in that state because I felt like everyone knew I was high. Then shyness kicked in, which is just a form of fear (I later learned that from the same preacher). I was not ready to stand in front of this large crowd of people. So I decided I was coming back the upcoming Tuesday. In my heart I felt freed from all the hurt and pain I stored up over the years, from others and from myself.

My friend that I grew up with (whom I called my cousin) was my first stop after church. I spent most of my time with him, his girlfriend and one of his roommates. I spent time with them especially if I was smoking marijuana and drinking. Upon my arrival I walked straight into the kitchen as I explained my recent encounter with God to them. I poured a small glass of Grey Goose liquor to get me started. While another person rolled the blunt, I continued my thoughts on getting saved and they began laughing at my so called encounter. The laughter was largely in part to the fact that I was currently smoking and drinking with them. I confidently told them that this was the last time I would partake in these types of activities. Of course they continued to laugh and that made me laugh because their doubt did not make me change everything that happened inside of me that Sunday morning. My mindset was...I'm out of this life. After smoking and taking a couple shots of liquor I wanted to go home to ponder on the church service and enjoy this overwhelming feeling of joy that I had never felt before that morning.

I was so excited that I went to my house in Jonesboro and called off of work and stayed home until that coming Tuesday to enjoy my new found peace. While at home I thought about all of the past events that led me up to this point in my life. I reflected on my childhood dilemmas, moving back and forth from state to state, my abusive marriage, getting arrested, and running into a guy I knew who informed me he became a minister. I told him I probably could never become a minister because of how much I cursed, had sex, smoked and drank. Then I told him I thought if I ever went to church...I would probably become a preacher. That was a scary thought at the time because I was also a professed Muslim, so I never thought much about going to church. At that time I enjoyed living in sin as it is referred.

Then I thought back to when I became a police officer and I decided I was not going to steal anymore. That changed to "Ok, I will not steal big ticket items anymore." A few months earlier in March of 2005 I took a road trip to Miami with my sister Kizzy, a friend from New York and one from Atlanta. My friend from New York and I were the only smokers so we had a smoke fest and topped it off with a whole lot of alcohol. When we (not including my friend from Atlanta) went shopping for swim suits we stole some tee shirts being that we were old boosting buddies. It was as if it was second nature. As I was involving myself I thought…I'm a police officer. I should not be doing this. I left whatever I did not shove into my purse, paid for my swim suit and headed for the car. When we arrived at the car I realized I left my camera in the boutique. I went back to get it with my sister but could not locate it. The cashier said she did not see any camera when she cleaned the dressing room and I knew she was lying. After I told her I was going to call the police to get my camera she started yelling, "You stole from the store, I saw all the hangers you left in the dressing room." I quickly advised her those hangers were already in there and she better get my camera at which point I informed her I was a police officer and I placed my badge on the counter. Then she reached under the counter and pulled out my camera. She told me to leave the boutique. I said, "Thank you" and we left. By the end of that trip, I lost that swim suit and knew stealing was not for me anymore big ticket or small ticket items.

My conscience was alive and you could not have one of those to successfully steal anything. My police car flipping over without any physical injuries and me sending my children to live with their father all raced through my mind as steps towards a more abundant life instead of obstacles of my past. On Tuesday I still felt high although that Sunday afternoon was the last time I smoked or drank. I knew that feeling came from the sermon. I did not want that feeling to leave from inside me but I knew if I did not go up to the front of the church this time that feeling was going to leave. I definitely did not want that. Fear tried to keep me from going again. Then the woman beside me asked if I wanted her to walk with me to the front. I said, "Yes", and we went together. Fear is not from God. We can

overcome fear by accomplishing whatever feels or seems
bigger than us. It can either stop you from getting to your
destination or it can compel you to achieve exactly what is
rightfully yours!

      After I got saved I learned that words people speak,
that I hear and images that I see are like seeds planted into
soil that has potential to grow into a tree of lifestyle. I
thought back to how Satan was attempting to plant seeds of
lesbianism in me. The earliest memories I have are when
I was about four or five and my female cousin and I were
caught naked in a closet. At that time we were simply doing
what we saw men and women do on television. When
I was about six or seven with another female cousin we
played house and we quickly grinded on top of one another.
Now I believe I knew it was wrong in some way because
the first time I did something of this nature I was yelled
at and made fun of by my older cousins. I do not recall
getting a spanking and I know I was not told why that was
morally inappropriate. When I was a pre-teen about 11 or
12 living with my mother, she had a live-in girlfriend after
my grandmother moved out. One day I made a comment
about her being gay while I was walking out the door, so
when I got outside she yelled out her bedroom window,
"The apple don't fall far from the tree." She was implying
that because she was unsure about who God made her, by
me being birthed through her I might not be sure either. I
lowly whispered to myself, "Yes it does." My mind began
to wonder was I gay because I did kiss my cousin in the
closet and my mother was gay. I wondered did my very
own mother who had not raised me know something about
me that I did not. My entire life at that time felt unfulfilled
or mysterious in many ways. I truly did not know who I
was. I kept saying one thing after my mother made that
statement, "I am not gay!"

When I was about 20 years old, this girl from around my grandmother's neighborhood came out of the closet about being a lesbian. Smoking marijuana was a major outlet for me and she smoked also. She invited me to smoke with her and I told my sister Kizzy and then that became a big joke on me. I was invited to a lesbian's house I thought for one reason but the real reason was because she really liked me. I never believed she was attracted to me in that way but I was not about to be proven wrong so of course I never made it to her house. On top of that, another girl Nisha and I went boosting or stealing clothes with was a lesbian and made a comment that she liked me. Why were gay people attracted to me? They were attracted to me because Satan was simply trying to get me to doubt my own sexuality. Satan had been attempting to water the seeds he planted in me as a child. When a seed is planted but is not watered, it will not grow. My mind was not willing to believe I was gay or curious in anyway. The memories of my early childhood experiences were blocked out intentionally by me. I never experimented with same sex and I never will.

My journey began with me continually saying Jesus is Lord and I love Him, while standing in front of my bathroom mirror. I had to get this new thought engraved in my heart because as a Muslim I was trained to believe opposite. My heart wanted to believe Jesus was the only way but my mind kept telling it…Jesus is just a man. I do not even remember how long I stood there in front of that mirror but when I was done my face was full of tears and when I said "Jesus" it was with shear confidence that He was my Lord, whom loves me!

Detaching "me" from my name and the many close sinful people in my life was my next step. Most people addressed me by my middle name "Jah-see" so I advised everyone including my parents and grandparents to, "Call me by my first name from now on." The name change was hard for everyone to adjust to but I had to stick out all the criticism and jokes, eventually they came around. I kept myself from visiting friends and even my family. For a lot of people that might seem stupid or even difficult. I read it in the bible after God had told me to do it and I wanted to obey Him. In the Bible Abram's name was changed to Abraham. The name change was to separate my past failures from my future promises. Names carry destiny and character traits so I knew God's destiny for my life was not assigned to my old name neither were my old characteristics. As with Abraham he had to leave his family, his way of living and the familiar things in character to him. I did the same. Most of my friends were still living in New York but we spoke often. I informed them my life was going to be lived for Jesus Christ now and we all pretty much ended all corrupt communication. Gossiping and any negative speech is corrupt; therefore my conversations were now about God. My friends had no interest in that.

For thirty days the Lord advised me to place a lock on my mouth. I was only allowed to speak on the issues of God, say hello, goodbye and answer questions for workplace situations was all I said for thirty days. With this exercise I learned how to think before I spoke and how to stay away from gossip and cursing, which came naturally. I had to explain to a few people that I could only speak about God whenever they kept trying to force a conversation. Also I changed my cellular number and slowly gave out my new number. This is a process I repeated around four times for a year. During my preteen years I became accustomed

71

to listening to sad love songs from my mother, which I stopped doing and began meditating on worship and gospel songs. My mother would play these sad love songs in her locked bedroom whenever she was getting high on drugs. If I ever planned on being in a real loving committed marriage I could not continue filling my mind with thoughts of hurt and pain from any past unproductive relationships.

The majority of my past time was spent smoking and drinking so when I stopped those activities I replaced it with repeatedly listening to sermons on CD and reading the Bible. I was totally disconnected from the world around me and I became engulfed with the things of God. Transforming from who I was to who God originally designed me to be was not easy for me to do but I purposed myself to do all that was necessary for it to happen. My friends, family and co-workers thought I had gone crazy. When a person begins to change sometimes the people around them have some form of concern or reservation about that new change. This happens especially when that new change eliminates them or forces them to change in some way.

I remember when the Father (God) shared with me to be at church for every service or event. One church service we had a guest speaker come in to teach us about our finances. Mainly he taught about God desiring for His people to lend money and not to borrow money. When my Pastor said the quickest way to get out of debt was to take the item back, I did exactly that. I was new to this lifestyle and how it worked. I was supposed to pray and ask God what He wanted me to do and how did He want me to go about doing it? I did not do that. I made up in my mind that I was not going to borrow from anyone ever again. I then got a plan to have my house supposedly rented out to a friend but that did not go through. Then my sister wanted me to supply the property to another venture which did not work out either. So I just abandoned the house after moving all of my stuff out. I was too impatient to wait on selling the house. My focus was getting free from debt as quick as possible. Then there was my new white car that I just borrowed fourteen thousand dollars for. It was a brand new loan that I did not want to take out in the first place. After my green station wagon was hit by a reckless driver the insurance company totaled out my vehicle. The accident happened when I was almost finished paying off that car loan. I was ignorant to the fact of having GAP insurance coverage, which would have paid for my new car. My new white car was on its way back to the dealership and I was headed for the bus line.

People thought that I was crazy because I removed myself from those debts but I only cared what God thought. I moved into an apartment close to my church and applied for a customer service job at the bank. Growing into this kind and gentle person I knew I was supposed to be was not going to happen being a police officer in the city. My character needed to be perfected and changed for the better. Plus in my heart, as a police officer I was disappointed with the way my supervisors neglected my hardship where my children were concerned. I was told that there were not any positions available during the shift that I desired. Then I began to notice a few people from my shift were transferred to the shift I seriously needed, that did not have hardships.

My Detroit co-worker from the police academy was just what I needed in my life. This was a turning point from who I was known as being, to a person no one ever thought I would become. She supported my change from day one and has continued to encourage me to be whatever I believed God called me to be. Leaving the police department was a critical financial decision. I was use to having money but it was time for me to trust God fully and lean completely on Him. With no mortgage, car note and a new lower paying job I was ready to focus on my new, debt free life with Jesus Christ. Being married again also became a new concept for me. One day the Lord told me I would be married next year and when I shared this information with a friend of mine at the time she questioned who it could be seeing as though I did not even have a boyfriend. I told her those were my exact thoughts but that is what God said and I believed Him. She moved back to New York before she could see God's miracle in my life.

There was one demon that haunted me more than the memory of a blood thirsty raging angry man or even the agony of abandonment by my mother. My soul ached for the senseless murder I had committed one early morning in late 2000 after returning to North Carolina…"a medical situation" (referenced in Chapter 3). In the past I had made some stupid mistakes but this one pierced me deep. The decision I made to abort my child was the most selfish and cruel mistake ever. I thank God for forgiving me of such an act. His love, grace and mercy ultimately allowed me to forgive myself. When I thought about the way an eight week old baby is sucked into a tube and their tiny legs, arms and head are being ripped from their helpless body…what kind of person does that to another? Then I had to answer and say, "A selfish, cruel, insensitive, weak, and uneducated person does that." That was me.

Thank God, He changed all of that with the blood of my Savior and Brother Jesus. He permitted me to become brand new without any residue of my past mistakes. That morning I walked into that clinic with a life inside of me.

As the woman in white pants and a short sleeved white shirt placed a needle in my arm, an older male walked in the room wearing glasses. He sat down in a rolling chair and began asking me questions as the medication began to consume my body. I could barely make out his questions and I remember he never looked at me. I wanted to look into his eyes for some strange reason. Then as I was awakening from the medication I was being carried or seemingly liked dragged to a waiting area. My eyes were so heavy. I tried to figure out my location? A woman brought me water to drink and as I looked around I saw women sitting in chairs looking like drug addicts. They were slouched down with their heads hanging and I imagine I was in the same posture. They stood me up and opened a door. Then a bright light rushed my face and I was taken to my vehicle by the father of my now dead baby.

We went back to his apartment he shared with a fellow soldier. The pain was excruciating and when I began to come alive again I realized what I had done. I realized I killed another human being. I began to scream and hit him continuously saying, "Why did you make me do this?" and "Why did I have to kill my baby?" I told him how I hated him for making me kill my baby. I wanted my baby and I could not have him. He just hugged me, gave me some medicine and did not say a word. I woke up later that day to an empty room. I could hear him downstairs with his roommate. I was reliving the morning event with tears of sobering and regret. I guess when I agreed to do it I thought he would change his mind. It did not really sink in what I had done until I had already done it. Then it was too late to change the outcome. It was too late for me to give my baby his life back. That senseless murder was a mental struggle for me. It took a lot of forgiving Tameeka and definitely the blood of Jesus to conquer that demon.

A new day approached and the past had to stay in the past because I was looking towards my future. Our church was having a Labor Day cookout that September of 2005, which I planned on attending. A new chapter was about to begin in my life that I was not primarily focusing on but God had me preparing for it.

Chapter 6
Brooklyn to the
Bible

*A*s I was awaiting the first sign of Jahlil and Jillian at the 2005 church cookout, this young lady asked me if I wanted to play a card game of spades. My answer was "Yes, of course". She probably noticed me looking at them whenever someone became excited at her table for winning. My younger sister Princess and her friend accompanied me to the cookout so I would not be alone. The reason for them coming was not accomplished because they went off on their own when we arrived and my children never showed up to the cookout.

A young light skinned gentleman I was playing spades with seemed a bit childish and obnoxious. He probably was not as annoying as I initially thought. Most of those feeling came from me not getting to see my children as I was expecting. On top of that, I did not have a vehicle any longer so I used Kizzy's car and I dreaded when I would have to begin riding MARTA (public transportation). I knew God told me to give up my vehicle so I did exactly that.

The Thursday following the cookout I decided to go to the marriage course at church. The Father (God) told me to attend. The first announcement for the course was made a month or two earlier. The course was fifty dollars to attend and I did not have it because of my new employment wages. When the last announcement was made there was no reference to the money so I decided to go. I got there late due to my new form of transportation (the bus and train). As I was walking into the sanctuary I was getting ready to sit in a particular row but changed my mind when I looked up and saw my children. They were there with their father and his fiancé. Instantly I became upset. I was not upset because he had someone. My mind was showing me that my children were not my children any longer and that hurt. I felt as though they were being taken from me. So I quickly spun around and sat in the row before them, right next to this young light skinned gentleman. The marriage course class was a blur and all I wanted to hear was "the end" so I could leave. When it was finally over I walked out so fast you would have thought I was a bolt of lightning.

That Sunday was the first Sunday I took the bus, train, another bus, and my children with me to church. Bathroom trips had to be made, breakfast had to be eaten, and snacks had to be prepared prior to leaving for the new and long adventure. This was the first time I had not been to the eight or ten am services at church. Today I was attending only the twelve pm service. Jahlil, Jillian and I had arrived a few minutes early to church so we were walking to McDonalds to sit down instead of us standing in the long line to get into church service. As I turned around towards the direction of McDonald's a voice saying "hello" greeted me. I was faced with a bright yellow shirt that was worn by this young light skinned gentleman with a big smile. I said "hello" back and was ready to continue going to my destination. I recognized the face of the man but I was not sure where I knew him from.

I was not into hanging out with men from the church. I did not want to hang out with anyone for that matter. My goal was to stay away from the cliques and not be overly socially known with everyone. Then the young man began to speak. He said, "What happened to you the other night, I wanted to say hello but you left so fast." I simply said nothing, I had no clue what he was referring to and I guess he knew that. He began to remind me by saying, "The other night at the marriage class when I turned around you were gone." "Oh yeah I had to catch the bus", was my response. I said that just so I could keep it short and not tell him the entire reason. He asked, "Where are you going, church is the other way?" When I turned around to explain the long line it was moving so we walked back to church together. He waited for me to sign the children into children's ministry and then we sat together and enjoyed Sunday service.

After church we kept talking and walking out of service. He escorted me to pick up my children. While we were there I ran into my children's father and we spoke privately. At that time we were still a bit friendly and he

inquired about the gentlemen I was with, "So y'all are
getting married?" I stated "why" just to keep him guessing.
Also that seemed like a great dream to be getting married
minus the fact that I did not know the guy. He then said, "I
seen y'all at the marriage class, so who is this guy?" "That
is not any of your business", I replied in a friendly manner.
When his fiancé came out of the children's ministry with her
daughter our conversation quickly ended as usual. After
getting my children the gentleman asked if I would like
a ride home. In times past I would never have taken any
guy up on this type of offer but then again this entire day
with him was not in my normal procedures of dealing with
people at church. My mouth said "yes" before my mind
could process all the objectives to the new scenario. On the
ride home he reminded me we were spade card partners
at the Labor Day cookout. He was not as silly as I thought
from that first encounter. Plus the fact that we did not have
to ride the buses and train was a blessing.

Tuesday night service to church began with the
Marta bus and train outbound but inbound I met up
with this nice young man again and he offered me yet
another ride home. I was beginning to think my mouth
was programmed to only respond "yes" in his case? Jahlil
and Jillian were with their father and when asked I had to
explain that situation to him. We had a very interesting
conversation the entire time it seemed. I was as curious as
to how he had moved from Baltimore Maryland to Atlanta
Georgia just for this church. It was like a movie in a sense
because I had only heard of people moving from all over the
world to be members of this wonderful church I was now
a part of. His faith in a God He had never seen and being
able to receive guidance to a whole new state from God, just
spoke volumes to me about how faithful and obedient he
was.

With him living amongst a generation of many
rebellious youth he seemed to be one in a million. In the
prior months I had met so many young men due to being a
police officer and I often spoke to them about their lives and
their faith. I never met one that was as faithful to their God
in action as they had claimed to be with their mouths. At that
time I was praying and believing for my ideal, dream man. I
had it written down on paper and I prayed for him every day.
However after meeting so many dead ends and getting weary
I decided to continue in my faith and be faithful to my God
who had begun to change my thinking and shape my new life
as He saw fit. I was not wondering, "Is he the one" any longer
or "He's cute, he could work out." I was allowing my future
husband to find me being faithful, committed and submissive
to our God and that was how I wanted to be found. When I
say faithful…I mean being at church every time it was open
for me to be there, reading daily for hours at a time, praying
for my future spouse, praying for others as well as myself, and
saying my daily confessions for my life out loud. If I wanted
to see change in my life I first had to know what God had
planned for me to have. Next I had to say exactly what it was
over and over every day. Then I had to truly believe what
I was committed to saying. Finally, I had to stick with the
necessary changes I made in my life. Therefore, the people
in my life now had to definitely line up with this new lifestyle
given to me from God.

Now when I say I was being submissive…I am
referring to doing the very task or assignment I was given
to do whether it was through a church sermon on CD
through the Pastors or ministers at church during any given
service. When they said we should pray for an hour every
day, I did it. I was determined to reprogram my mind
from Brooklyn to the Bible. So if the Bible said I must love
those that despitefully use me, I was seeking out ways and

opportunities to do just that. Growing up with my father
I became very self-reliant or independent and I never felt
like I needed a man to lead me in any direction especially
his own direction. Therefore, I had to practice being
submissive to a man. I used God and my Pastor to start
with.

I knew from past relationships that I was not a person
to congratulate, encourage, esteem or really respect a man. I
was going to change all of that with this new relationship with
God. I was determined to thank God and say loving words
toward Him and sing love songs to Him, this was my mission.
Also whatever my Pastor said at church I did just that. By
making all these adjustments in my life I was preparing
myself for the husband, children, career, friends etc. that I
knew God said belonged to the new me...Tameeka.

Now that I was becoming the new Tameeka after
months of reprogramming my mind here comes this young
man and his strong faith. This is just what I had been praying
for in a husband. I thought he was a nice looking young
man but I was not thinking he was "the one" or could be "the
one" for that matter. When we got to my place we sat in his
black 1992 Buick LeSabre talking about how he gave his life
to Christ. He then began telling me he was originally going
to move to Atlanta with his girlfriend. So I assumed they
were still a couple. I asked him when was she going to move
to Atlanta and he said before he left Baltimore they broke up.
However he kept making remarks about his girlfriend who he
supposedly had broken up with. They seemed like a couple
that were meant to be together from the stories he told me in
regards to their relationship. I remembered thinking, "She
was a lucky girl". Later I learned there is no such thing as luck
but in life there is the favor and blessing of God on a person's
life. That night I went into my place after sitting in his car in

amazement for four or five short hours. The next Tuesday was like an instant replay. Here we were again in his car talking for hours that went by so quickly. We talked about our childhood and he told me he has been brushing his teeth before he goes to bed at night since he was a child. My teeth on the other hand were brushed only in the morning since I was a child. As I was in my bathroom that night, the Lord told me to brush my teeth before I go to bed. I looked around and said, "Huh, that's what he does not me." God simply reminded me of our earlier conversations. He asked me, "You said you could submit, right?" I said, "Yes, but he's not my husband." God asked me, "Do you want to submit or not?" With a smile my response was, "Okay, I'll brush my teeth before I go to bed."

I really appreciated the way God gave me a task in response to what I said in order to allow me to prove myself, to me. For a quick moment I thought, "Was he the guy I was going to marry next year?" Then I purposed myself not to assume this young man was to be my husband. Maybe I did not want to get disappointed or maybe it was the girl he left in Baltimore. He drove me home every Sunday and Tuesday after church and he picked me up some Sunday mornings. Every time we spoke he intrigued me even the more. Men that I met prior were just not like this guy. He was very candid and I was eager to learn any additional history about him.

Roy Jones Jr. and Antonio Tarva were having a boxing match for the third time. My sister Kizzy and I decided to go watch the fight with the young man named Rodney and his friend out in Roswell Georgia. During the car ride Kizzy surprisingly asked, "You like him?" I quickly said, "No." She asked, "He like you?" I thought that would be nice if he did. I said, "No, I don't think so".

He was attractive to me by this time but I did not
think it was appropriate to be attracted to someone if
you were saved. Yeah, I was really deep. I thought liking
someone was lustful and I thought you had to get married
to who God chose then learn to love that person. The
four of us were sitting at the table of this overly crowded
Sports Bar and Grill. His friend was more interested in me
than Rodney was. It seemed as though Rodney was more
curious about my sister while totally ignoring me. Was I
actually getting jealous? I had become accustomed to him
giving me his attention that I must say I was jealous. The
fight was surprisingly not the Roy Jones Jr. performance I
expected. I was a fan of Roy Jones Jr. so of course when he
lost I was not happy about it. As we all walked to our cars
and made small talk I asked if they wanted to take some
pictures. Now finally, this was what I was used to from
him…attention…and I wanted the moment to stand still
and breathe this breath of enjoyment. That was a breath I
could breathe all day.

When Kizzy and I began our journey home as
usual we did not know which direction to go on Interstate
285. 285 is a circle and we were not frequent users of
this particular highway. I then text messaged Rodney
for directions. He was just as clueless as us. He just
moved here from Baltimore, why did I expect him to
know? It turned out we went the extremely long way
around Interstate 285, so we continued texting each other.
Somehow the question came up, "Do you like me?" I put
the question back on him before I answered it and made a
fool of myself. That seemed like the longest response time
of a text message ever but it was worth the wait to read
his "yes" answer. I felt like a teenager all over again with
butterflies in my stomach and an uncontrollable smile from
ear to ear.

Now that we expressed our like for one another we seized every opportunity to inquire more details on each other. My first confession was asking him was it okay to be attracted to someone? Although I did like him I was not completely at peace with the idea of being attracted to him. He assured me that God gives us the option to choose our spouse and as long as lustful or sexual thoughts were not occurring, liking someone was okay before being married. The thought crossed my mind…was he attracted to me while he was awaiting his old girlfriend to come to her senses and move to Atlanta? They had just broken up about four or five months prior. He guaranteed me he was over her and he had been given clear instructions from God to just be friends with her.

By September 30th I was graduating from my New Members class and I asked him to accompany me to the "New Members Fiesta". He accepted my invitation and we had a great time. I even participated in the dance line that circled the room. The only time I danced in the past I was either drunk or high on marijuana.

I had been saved for six months and I had not received my free gift of speaking in tongues. I was getting upset and that was not helping me pray in tongues any quicker so I decided to confide that information to Rodney. Speaking in tongues or praying in tongues is simply a way to communicate directly to God without Satan knowing what you are praying. At times you might not know either. This is the perfect prayer and it brings you a peace that people who use drugs might be able to relate to. When a person first gets high on a drug like heroin the first high is so relaxing (although I have never personally used heroin). The relaxation they experience is like a peace of mind and body. Every time they get high after that, it is like a chase to get that same feeling of peace again which they never can get. Praying in tongues is better because it is not temporary and can give you peace in its entirety. Praying in tongues provides you peace of mind, body and soul. When a person is born again the Holy Spirit comes on the inside of them and they are filled with the love of God.

While I was walking home after my bus and train ride from work, Rodney and I were on the phone and he gave me instructions to my desired gift. He told me to pray in tongues I should think about something I really wanted God to answer and begin to speak without thinking about how it sounds, and then I would start praying in tongues. I had to focus in on God and believe I could receive my free gift and just like he said it would happen it did. When I initially gave my life to Christ I was filled with the Holy Spirit, but when I received my gift to speak in tongues I was baptized with the Holy Ghost.

I was so happy. I kept praying, laughing and crying. It was a long wait and I did not want to stop. I thought what if I was not able to pray in tongues again? So I stopped for a second, then started again it was beautiful! This Rodney character was being used by God to deliver blessings to me and I enjoyed every one of them.

After being seen together at church all the time people began asking us were we dating? In our discussions that did not come up so my response to people was "no". Since people brought that to our attention we had to figure out or decide what exactly we were doing. First we had to express what our definition of dating was. My definition of dating was two people that were attracted to each other that went out in public together and they were getting to know each other to eventually get married. Then I asked

Rodney his definition and he said, "That's my definition too, so I guess we are dating." After I mentally processed his response it hit me, "We're getting married!" He was driving me home at the time and I had a big smile on my face. It was a good thing he was paying more attention to the road than my silly grin. This was a fast moving relationship. I just met him on Labor Day and now it's October and we're dating to be married. I know it had a lot to do with us defining everything and being completely honest with one another. We wanted to be clear on what we meant when we spoke. For example in our conversations I would ask him his definition of a husband and a wife. He would ask me stuff like what is my definition of being a friend or he'd inquire how often I will cook for my husband and children. Doing this every time we spoke allowed us to grow together at a rapid pace.

My first scheduled baptism did not work out. I lost track of time talking with the church New Members volunteer staff. I was explaining to them what department I wanted to serve and how I first came to the church. Whether I spoke to them or not I would not have made the baptism, I forgot to bring a change of clothes I later realized. For my second baptism attempt I borrowed my sister's car to make it on time and when I went outside the tire to her car was flat. I started crying because of course I did not want to miss being baptized again. I called a girl from church and got a ride from her. After she got lost and the baptism was scheduled to have started I got even more upset. I had forgotten the directions to the baptism at home but the Lord got us there. Don't ask me how. I had problem after problem. I was very upset when I finally got there. I thought it was finished. Thank God it was not and another pleasant surprise was Rodney was assisting the Minister with all the baptisms. So he baptized me in addition to helping me receive the gift to pray in tongues. Every day that went by I grew to love him more and more.

By January 2006 we began to start saving money for our wedding. It was all beginning to come together like God said. While working as a bank teller I met an interesting man who would later play a special role in my near future. In comes a man looking for his ATM card he had left in the ATM machine the day prior. The teller next to me said he was a mean guy so she quickly pretended to be too busy for customers. I greeted him with a "hello" and asked him what I could do for him today. He told me about his card situation and I advised him when I find it I'd call him because I was the person that handled incoming ATM cards. Later that day I did receive his card, so I looked up his number in our computer system and left him a message. The next day he came in and I gave him the card. We had a brief conversation about him being a chef for the restaurant next door.

About an hour or two later a guy came in with a platter tray asking for Tameeka. It was a platter of food from the restaurant next door the chef sent me. What a nice thank you that was. It was such a big platter, I gave food to everyone who worked at the bank and I had food left over to take home. I was determined to show the teller next to me the man was not as mean as she thought. Through me being genuinely friendly and loving with my interactions with him, he in turn was nice toward me. The other teller got to see this when he sent me the platter. After Rodney and I did not find a nice practical place to have our wedding ceremony, the restaurant next door came to mind while one day talking with the chef at the bank. He told me weddings were allowed and to let him know if and when I wanted to use the restaurant.

November 04, 2006 was the date we agreed on. When we had about two hundred dollars saved we decided

we should sow it in order to reap the full amount to pay
for the wedding. Sowing is when you believe God has
given you a promise of something and you place or give a
financial gift to a person or ministry. For example, if I was
watching a Pastor on TBN (Trinity Broadcasting Network)
and he said, "God is telling me a woman needs her left ear
healed", if my spirit leaps or if I believe he is talking about
me, I can send that Pastor a financial gift in agreement with
that healing. The gift is not to get the healing. The gift is
however an act of agreement to what God said through the
Pastor. "Why give money?" is the question a lot of people
have. Money is usually the most important possession to
people, so to truly exert your trust in God and release what
is the most precious shows faith. For most people money is
the most precious. If God says give something else, do that.
The important thing is you do what God is telling you to do.
Up until this point my walk with the Lord had been on
the straight and narrow. The only desire I had left to see
happen was the return of my children to my custody. By
this point their father was getting financial support from
me and borrowed money from me a couple times as well.
In return he would keep me from seeing the children
depending on his mood. He had disregarded his past
statement that I could get them anytime I wanted….I guess
that was said so he could ease me into releasing custody.
None the less my cries to the lord seemed to go unheard. I
still went to church, prayed daily, said my daily confessions,
I loved people that didn't love me etc., but inside I began
to resent God. My mind constantly thought about how
much I missed the children, "why would You allow this to
continuously happen to me?" I asked God on numerous
occasions with no return response. Had I done something
wrong to deserve this inner knotting pain I could not
soothe? I repeatedly told myself yes Tameeka you choose
to send them to live with him, but that was before you

knew Christ, you didn't know any better forgive yourself
and move on with your life. I would cry myself to sleep
some nights, fast from eating food and pray just for a sign
to let me know change was going to come. A breakthrough
or a break out of this current custody situation began to
consume my mind. As I went deeper into my self-pity I
knew I had to release this stress I placed on myself. I knew
I wasn't leaving the church, however being there without
seeing results made it difficult to go and enjoy it fully.

One night I was at Rodney's apartment we were
laying on his bed talking in the dark then after a soft kiss
on the lips my resentment for God turned to revenge. No I
wasn't leaving church, but I wasn't living church this night
either. I wanted to get God's attention one way or another.
The sex wasn't the focus for me. It was about repaying God
for the lack of listening as I saw it. If He wasn't going to
answer my prayer I wasn't going to completely live like He
asked! Although I felt bad about doing it afterwards and I
repented or asked God to forgive me I allowed myself to
do it again awhile after and this went on for a few months
before we decided to reset our boundaries, stick to them
and love the lord with our mind, soul and body. We also
had to conquer this lust demon before getting married as
we did not want this to be an issue later on in our marriage.
So no more kisses on the lips as we already knew where that
road led.

Chapter 7
Lasting Love

he big day was coming soon and we still did not have all of the money for the wedding yet. We knew this was happening because we sowed the two hundred dollars and the lack of finances was trying to make us doubt God's ability to provide for our big day. We just made up in our heart and mind that God would make a way for us and we would have what we needed no matter what it looked like. Now it is November 3rd…my grandmother already paid for my wedding dress, my mother bought the cake, a young lady paid for my nails to get done, another young lady did my makeup, and we still did not have all of the money to pay for the restaurant. We had over fifteen friends and family members come in from out of town and over sixty guests total. Panic was not an option. We continued to believe God would come through for us.

The first celebration was the night before at the Fox bar and grill in Buckhead where we paid an unexpected one hundred dollars for the event. Finally the big day is here, it is November 4th 2006 and we still needed more money.

We proceeded with our ceremony, which was beautiful. Before I met my father in the hallway I took a moment to soak in where I was this time last year and how far God had brought me to get me to this today. It was amazing to go from an abusive marriage, no self esteem, a single mother of two, using drugs, being bitter, using sex as a form of love, being a thief among other things…to now being saved, Holy Ghost filled, drug free, joyous and about to become the wife to a very handsome and humble man. I had to hold back the tears of thanksgiving before I messed up my lightly made up face. Showtime was approaching so I went to meet my father who greeted me with a hug and kiss he gently placed my arm under his as we began to walk. The assigned tables were pushed apart and all of the guests were standing in front of them with cameras and smiles as my father and I slowly walked by.

Rodney and I said our vows of prosperity and unconditional love. We joined in a covenant with God to help make each other a great success. The minister held a lit white candle as Rodney and I joined our candles simultaneously to his. They were now all lit to signify our union with God in our marriage. Finally we were given the instruction to kiss as husband and wife, which we gladly did.

The tables were arranged back into place for the delicious menu of jerk chicken, macaroni and cheese, peas and rice, and vegetable rolls. It was pretty much a West Indian menu as my husband says. After everyone finished eating people began to bring me gift bags, money and envelopes stuffed with money inside. Then the bill came for the restaurant and it was five hundred dollars less than the initially agreed price. Praise the Lord we came in not knowing how we were going to completely pay for the restaurant to being blessed with hundreds of dollars in financial gifts and a decrease in price. We believed God was going to show up on our behalf and He did! His Word says He will do exceedingly abundantly above all we could ask or think and that is exactly what He did for us. The chef was actually the restaurant's head chef and he was used by God to give us that wonderful price at such an elegant well known Atlanta restaurant. Cinderella and Prince Charming so to speak was now Mr. and Mrs. Rodney Williamson. The event was festive, unique and complete with a delicious menu.

Subsequent to our first few months of marital bliss our knowledge of 1Corinthians13 and every one of the marriage counseling classes were about to be tested. Around maybe our fifth or sixth month of marriage I was still making decisions based on my emotions although I was born again. Most of my life I was emotionally dependent on someone in one way or another and when I literally did not "feel" like working anymore because I was pregnant now, I decided not to return to work the next day. Here I was with a brand new husband and "I" decided to quit my job.

Yes, that was a very selfish and emotional choice on my part. My husband's response was calm initially. We then began to argue, which led to extended verbal and physical communication breaks. My first instinct was to leave and go back to New York for awhile and then I remember my husband telling me I ran away from my problems in the past. I truly desired to transform my old reactions so I chose to stay in spite of him now wanting a divorce. One day I told him if he wanted a divorce and I wanted an abortion and surprisingly he agreed. Here we are two born again believers and we actually agreed to kill another human being. Not to mention it was our very own creation, it was our child. We were both insane at that point especially me because I knew what struggles that decision entangled. We believed the Bible…any life is important and should never be willingly taken under any circumstance. Self defense is another act all in itself but murder is murder.

Soon after that, my heart began to ache and mourn the child that I in fact did abort. It was as if I was reliving that day all over again. Yes, I had been forgiven by God and I had forgiven myself but if I would have in fact followed through with the murder of this child, I mentally or spiritually was not going to be able to bounce back from that this time. So I was given the opportunity to hear God tell me my baby boy was in heaven and I was already forgiven. That night my Father placed a shield of peace and healing over my heart and mind. So needless to say, an abortion was never going to be an option for me again! My husband did not want any part of me, actually he told me to get out and leave his apartment.

By the end of that extremely long day, I packed my suitcases and departed in a taxi cab to a friend's house. What in the world was going on with my marriage? I remembered learning an important lesson after I removed my wedding ring…a person's actions expresses what that person believes. There was a very critical question God asked me as I sat down on the bed next to my over packed bags…"Do you want to make your marriage work?" "Yes", I responded with tears on my face, "Yes, I do not want to quit or run away anymore." I chose to stay married and because of that I had to act married. Married people wear rings as a symbol of their covenant. After that important lesson, I placed the ring back on my finger and I turned the television to the TBN praise-a-thon and it was as though every preacher spoke about marriage. They prayed for marriages being restored and I cried, prayed and thanked God. This program was tailor made for me. I did not say anything verbally about what was happening in my marriage to my friend. When a thought tried to enter my mind about my husband kicking me out or how he left me while I'm pregnant, I quickly said out loud, "Nothing shall by any means hurt me" (Luke 10:19), or I would say, "I love him and he loves me." Two days of this encouraged me to continue trusting God's power of restoration for our marriage.

On the third morning I went to our apartment while he was at work to make him dinner then I was going to leave before he came home. As I approached the kitchen I stopped at the counter to read a hand written note for me from my husband. It read…"Tameeka please come home. I miss you and we will talk later. Love, Rodney". My knees buckled and I began to weep. I wanted to stay but I could not. The meal never got made and I left the note intact. For some reason I did not want him to know I was there, it was like he expected my visit. I blocked the number to my location and called his place of employment just to hear his voice those three days but I never said a word. Later that night after rereading his note in my mind I called him just to hear his voice and he knew it was me on the other end of the phone. He simply said, "Where are you? I'm coming to get you." He arrived shortly after that to pick me up. When we got home he unpacked my bags and held me tight every night for about a week. There was not any more running from my problems. I chose to stay and change all that was wrong with me. Finally, I matured. Knowing what to do was one thing…applying what I knew was a whole other task.

Marriage is a tremendous adventure full of laughs, hugs, learning, and self adaptation, which equals a great deal of work. Our opportunity to sign divorce papers presented itself, but we decided to stand on the Word of God instead. From that moment on our marriage has grown stronger because under no condition will we disconnect our love towards each other again.

About six months later on November 3rd 2007 we welcomed our beautiful baby girl Gabriel home. Rodney, Jahlil, Jillian and I decided to go to the movies. When we arrived my stomach began to ache. Aches for me were really contractions. After the movie we went home where I endured more aches. To help ease the pain Jillian placed some fruit in a bowl for me, which she ended up eating. We left for the hospital shortly after and as I sat in the wheelchair awaiting a room. I advised the nurse the baby was coming. I guess they were used to hearing false alarms because she ignored my information the first time. So I went to the restroom to check myself and sure enough the baby was coming down. I told Rodney and he told the nurse again, she still did not respond. When another nurse came out we informed her and when she saw that the baby was actually coming she got behind my wheelchair and ran to an open room. The on call doctor had not arrived yet but the baby did not care anything about that. I told the nurse I needed to push and she asked me to wait until the doctor arrived if I could. When I said I would not be able to wait she called in another doctor and I began to push. After three pushes, she was born, wiped off then placed in my arms. We all enjoyed that night at the hospital with the new baby. Jahlil and Jillian enjoyed spending the night at the hospital getting an unlimited supply of cheese cracker, juices, graham crackers and even rice krispy treats.

We have had other challenges in our marriage, mainly due to having a blended family. Jahlil and Jillian were still physically living with their father and his new family. Their father slowly began decreasing his church attendance around the time I met Rodney, which allowed him to regress to his old ways. When I married Rodney his aggression grew stronger towards me then towards Rodney. After numerous church counseling sessions, he still refused to operate as a godly blended family with us. The Bible talks about many being called, but few being chosen. My husband, children and I are definitely chosen of God. It is a must to change the way you think to the way God thinks, which we purposefully do on a daily basis. I have come to learn that a lot of people say that they love Jesus but to love Him is to obey Him. To obey Him is to fashion your life after Him. To fashion your life after Christ you must have boundaries, commitment, consistency, self- control, be teachable, and be diligent.

Whenever Jahlil and Jillian's father came around we were not surprised at any of his obscene actions. We have endured him cursing at us, yelling in my husband's face, kicking on our door, stealing our cellular phone after choking and pushing me at Jillian's 2007 graduation while I was four months pregnant with Gabriel, keeping the children away from us, lying to the child support office about monies he did receive, scratching our vehicle, causing me to go to jail for three days while being pregnant with Gabriel, breaking our home's flood lights, pulling out a gun on my husband, disrespecting our property, countless attacks on my character in the many court appearances, and getting me arrested again for five days for the same accusation of not paying him child support when we both had the children an even amount of time.

In summary, that is the law working on behalf
of Satan through a man. The last court hearing we were
advised to turn in our request for the custody changes.
When it was all said and done, the new custody order came
in the mail and not one request we asked for was granted.
Walter and his lawyer looked as if they had won that day
because the current visitation arrangements were changed
to everything they requested and in court the judge threw
out our request for cancelling child support. No more week
with us and week with them during the summer, no more
six days with us in a two week period and eight days with
them. The children had to stay with them the last month
of the summer until after school began. Then they would
only come home with us every other weekend from Friday
to Monday morning. Plus we were ordered to pay his court
fees. Laugh, just laugh is what we had to do. It was a swift
blow from Satan, but it was not deadly and by no means will
we give in or turn coward because of this.

We still trust God to show up and now perform a
miracle on our behalf. God knows the desires of our hearts.
He knows we live for Him and He definitely knows where
those children will be raised up to live out His word. When
it looks like you lost that is when God gets all the glory
for the victory that is coming. When you cannot claim by
your own strength or knowledge that you made this victory
happen, God shows you He is the great I AM. Jahlil and
Jillian will in the end be with us and we continue to trust
God and His Word without fear of defeat! I could probably
go on and on about all of the other attacks Satan has done
through that man but I would rather tell you what we did to
keep from perhaps killing someone out of rage.

Through all of that Rodney and I have grown in our
godly character and in our marriage. We completely believe

the Word of God and it says, "Many are the afflictions of the righteous: but the LORD delivereth him out of them all." (Psalm 34:19) We have learned to trust the Father and love any person that deliberately does wrong to us. Turning the other cheek several times was accomplished. Not saying if he hits me on one cheek, turn to the other side and let him hit that cheek. Turning the other cheek means if he hits you on one cheek or if he so happens to hit you on the other cheek too, you as a disciplined person of Jesus should simply walk away. It is one thing to say you believe the Word of God and it is another thing to live it out in obedience and in its entirety. When you continuously conquer the enemy also known as Satan and when you mature into the Bible's definition of love then you can confidently and truly say you believe the Word because you live it.

I thought I knew God loved me. Through going to court, listening to people lie on me, being arrested, and the pressure it put on my marriage all positioned me to trust God. It all helped me to strengthen my faith and develop my character. Today I know without a shadow of a doubt that my Father loves me and He is the Most High God! Sure there were times that I wanted to quit and cave in to the traps. When people treat you like dirt and continue to speak evil of you even while you are being kind takes self-control. We had to constantly repeat the scriptures in our mind and out loud in the mist of these obstacles. On a daily basis we had to meditate on the Word of God. For example if we needed strength to turn the other cheek, we would read the scripture Luke 6:29 over and over. We would plan out how we should respond to physical confrontations. We also would repeatedly listen to sermons about the characteristics of love. All of these steps helped us to grow in our godly character of love. Along with trusting in God, this enabled us to have victory, time after time.

With three beautiful children and Dominic on the way, we have created a new generation that is not subject to our past mishaps because of God's love. Being a born again woman of God is not the pinnacle of my story. This is only the beginning of my rectification… of a life's long journey with Christ. By confronting the past that shaped me, it empowered me to write this book. This book is a "thank you" to everyone for their part in this epic. Everything from my growing pains to my lasting love, whether it was from others or from me, I can confidently say that ALL IS FORGIVEN!

Without the forgiveness given to me by Jesus Christ I could have never fully forgiven & forgotten all the wrong things done to me nor could I truly forgive myself for the wrong things I did. If you want to live a life of forgiveness I urge you to surrender yourself to the One that has already forgiven you.

Jesus Christ is your open door to that life, if you would like for Jesus to be Lord of your life repeat this prayer and allow the love of God to fill your heart an enable you to forgive whomever or whatever:

Father I confess with my mouth and believe in my heart that You have forgiven me of my sins, I ask that You fill me with the wisdom on how to forgive others & I thank You that today I have chosen to succeed with You! In Jesus' name. Amen.

Thank You!

First and most importantly, I must give thanks and praise to my Lord and Savior Jesus Christ. Without whom I would probably be dead or in jail and this book would have a different ending. Thank you for the cleansing blood!

To Rodney, the man that holds my hand with a smile as I journey from faith to faith. You have inspired me with your achievements, you have encouraged me with sincere words from the heart and you have confronted me when I was not being the woman God called me to be. Thank you for your true unconditional and loyal love, it compels me to overly achieve all God has for me to do. Selah!

To our children Jahlil, Jillian, Gabriel and Dominic continue on the road we have reared you to walk…daily with Jesus. I love you all and I am honored God chose me to be your mother.

To my father Curtis Arthur, I thank you for being a diligent provider, for your stern parenting and all those lengthy conversation as a teenager. To my mother Angela Carter, thank you for showing me what it looks like to win BIG (to be more than a conquer) when it seems like everyone has counted you out. I love you both. To my other parents Roderick and Phyllis Williamson, you both have welcomed me and the children into your family, and I am deeply thankful. I love you both.

To my brother Ishmel and my sisters Quatavia, Akilah, Princess, Georgia, Shelina, Nisha, Kizzy and Rakee Williamson thank you all for being joint heirs with me, love y'all.

A special thanks to my grandmother Wilma Brown, Rosalyn, Theandre and Kimberlyn: Thanks for grooming me for the future. We became a family because of the way you all strengthen, enlightened and molded me into a young woman *and I thank you tremendously for your devoted time and love.*

To The Kirkland's: Thank you for the excellent wedding assistance. To my church family: we are the blueprint church that provides 5 star services! Keep growing with me. Special thank you to: Mrs. Tanya Johnson, the Hightower family & Mr. Lamont Hart kudos to you all and your excellent God given talents!

To "The Silas Project" participants I say EARLY RELEASE love you all!

Thank you to Mrs. "D" who walked with me to the altar in 2005!

Finally I want to thank my Pastors Mason and Twyla Betha for obeying the call on their lives and teaching me how to live this abundant life with Christ! I love you both.

www.ingramcontent.com/pod-product-compliance
Lightning Source LLC
Chambersburg PA
CBHW060358050426
42449CB00009B/1800